MORNINGS
with
BARNEY

THE TRUE STORY OF AN EXTRAORDINARY BEAGLE

Dick Wolfsie

Skyhorse Publishing

Skyhorse Publishing books may be purchased in bulk at special discounts for sales promotion, corporate gifts, fund-raising, or educational purposes. Special editions can also be created to specifications. For details, contact the Special Sales Department, Skyhorse Publishing, 307 West 36th Street, 11th Floor, New York, NY 10018 or info@skyhorsepublishing.com.

Skyhorse˚ and Skyhorse Publishing˚ are registered trademarks of Skyhorse Publishing, Inc.˚, a Delaware corporation.

Visit our website at www.skyhorsepublishing.com.

10 9 8 7 6 5 4 3 2 1

Paperback ISBN: 978-1-62087-193-5

Library of Congress Cataloging-in-Publication Data

Wolfsie, Dick.
    Mornings with Barney : the true story of an extraordinary beagle / by Dick Wolfsie.
        p. cm.
IS BN 978-1-60239-353-0 (alk. paper)
1. Barney (Dog) I. Title.
PN1992.8.A58W654 2008
791.4502'80929—dc22
        2008034295

Printed in the United States of America

This book is dedicated to Mary Ellen and Brett. Without their patience with Barney—and their love for me—this story would have ended where it began.

Beagle on the Doorstep

Had I lost my mind? Why would a seasoned television reporter do something like this? I shuffled the beagle into the backseat of my old 1978 Chevy Monte Carlo, adjusted the rearview mirror to keep him visible, and hoped that this approach to solving the problem was only temporary.

For the past week the dog had been an intruder in our home. And all of us had been his victims. "Victims" is not the word I would have chosen, but my wife, Mary Ellen, and my three-year-old son, Brett, decided it was the appropriate label. It was hard to argue.

As I drove to work, I checked the mirror constantly. The little interloper had gnawed through his new polyester-nylon-blend leash. Did I know at the time that this trip would signal the beginning of a television legend in Central Indiana? No, I wasn't that smart. I had only one goal in mind: I wanted to save my marriage from this home wrecker.

The day I found the dog, I began my routine as I had every workday for the four previous months with the 3:30 AM buzz of the alarm. Even though I was a morning person, this new early wake-up time seemed contrary to the U.S. Constitution's ban on cruel and unusual punishment.

I opened the front door of our Tudor home to get a sense of the weather. A few of my television segments in the winter were shot with me outside, standing in snow and ice, telling people (as though they were morons) to drive slowly. I had great respect for our meteorologist's overnight predictions, but there was nothing more accurate than getting smacked in the face with a frigid blast of midwestern January wind if you wanted to assess the current conditions.

It was bone-aching cold that morning, but before I turned back from the front door to retrieve still another layer of protection I had left on the sofa, a pair of soulful brown eyes stared up at me from the bushes. This was not the first time a beautiful pair of peepers had gotten me in trouble, but in the past, the glances had always been attached to a body with two comely legs, not four.

Then it began: a howl that I would hear on a daily basis for the next twelve years. That first time wasn't just a howl, it was a plea to open my home to a complete stranger, one who had possibly lived a good deal of his life on the streets of Indianapolis and now needed to find a place he could destroy all his own.

On closer inspection, I realized the creature was a beagle. Black and white and brown. And shivering. Despite his disheveled look, he appeared well-fed, so I assumed he had run away from a neighbor's home. But he had no collar. What he did have was a certain presence. For more than a few seconds, I just watched him as he vied for my attention. His head didn't budge but his eyes followed my every move. Then he sat up on his hind legs and flicked his paw at me, like he was giving me a high five. I was captivated. At the time it struck me as odd, the effect he had on me. Now I understand.

I couldn't leave the little guy out in the cold. I picked him up and was surprised he was so compliant. *What a sweet dog,* I thought. My wife and son were still asleep upstairs, and waking them seemed unnecessary. I placed the dog on the rug in the living room and he was content . . . so tired from his apparent journey that I figured it was safe to just leave him there to rest for a few hours. My reporting obligations for the early morning show usually got me home by 7:30, almost a half-hour before the rest of the Wolfsies crawled out of bed. By the time I got back, I could explain the dog's presence and decide what to do next. What was the harm in that?

I'm an idiot.

That morning I reported live from the Boat, Sport & Travel Show, an annual event in Indianapolis that features everything for the sportsman and adventurer. One of my guests was a lumberjack who entertained the crowds with log-rolling and tree-chopping demonstrations. At the end of the program, as I prepared to head back, I told him about the beagle pup I had found on my doorstep. He flashed me a big, toothy smile and said, "Are you serious? You left a stray beagle alone, unattended in your house?" And with that, he gathered his tools, climbed into his sedan, and sped off. In Grimm's Fairy Tales, the woodsmen were good with foreshadowing, so I quickly headed home.

Fifteen minutes later, I pulled into our driveway. Lights were on all through the house. Not a good sign at this hour. Despite the chilly temperature, the door was slightly ajar, so I peeked in, hoping to see that the dog was still asleep on the rug. I hoped he had not crawled up onto the couch.

Yeah, he was on the couch . . . what was left of it, along with what was left of the shredded pillows. I stepped inside. The curtains had been literally yanked off their rods, and one designer high-heel shoe, minus the heel but with a new fashionable hole in the toe, sat in the middle of the kitchen floor. A corner of the dining room rug had been ripped up, and the kitchen trash can had been knocked over, with the contents distributed across the floor. Later, after an extensive inventory, we concluded that a lot had been ingested, as well.

Incredibly, he had not had an accident. What a good dog!

As I surveyed the wreckage, my son, Brett, descended the stairs with a beheaded teddy bear and an unstuffed lion, more casualties of the dog's multilevel tirade. Tears rolled down Brett's cheeks. He stared at the beagle, then shot a glance at his decapitated menagerie.

"Daddy, can we *not* keep him?"

Brett was not a dog person. Our cats, Benson and Lindsay, had been family members for several years and Brett was comfortable with their unassuming, laid-back style. The two felines barely acknowledged each other, save an occasional spat when they encountered the food bowl at the same time. In just the couple of hours that the new dog had occupied our house, the cats had already formed an alliance to protect their turf. They began tormenting the trespasser by pawing and hissing at him. I don't think Barney had much experience with cats and was confused by the pandemonium he had created, clearly perplexed by the notion that another living creature might not take to him at first sight.

Mary Ellen was understandably a little stressed, not sure if this interloper might have a mean streak, so when Barney finally had the courage to lunge at one of the cats in self-defense, my wife let out a scream that frightened both me and the beagle half to death. Brett, in the meantime, had grabbed a pillow from the couch and was swatting wildly at the dog.

All this chaos was enough evidence for my son: we didn't need a dog, especially one that represented a serious threat to the relative tranquility in our home.

Mary Ellen zeroed in with a piercing gaze that I was unfamiliar with. After all these years, I don't remember her exact words, but I do remember that the expression on her face was one I was not familiar—or comfortable—with. Mary Ellen is a loving, giving, caring person, but she does not tolerate chaos. When she plans our vacations, she peruses maps, analyzes the landscape, and consults books for details of the climate and culture. "Are we planning a vacation or an invasion?" I always ask her. I was afraid what she was planning now.

No, the beagle had not made a good first impression. Mary Ellen offered me the "opportunity to return him." She sure knew how to phrase things. This seemed like a reasonable request. Wait a second—I didn't know where he came from.

"What's his name?" Mary Ellen asked.

"I have no idea. We just met."

That morning I had done a segment at a new café in Danville, Indiana, patterned after the old Andy Griffith Show. I guess the name Barney (as in Fife) was on my mind. He could have ended up being an Opie or a Floyd or even a Griffith. No, he was going to be Barney.

Mary Ellen, then an administrator at Community Hospital in Indianapolis, headed off for work and offered to drop Brett off at preschool, which was normally my job. She never said it, but I think she expected me to deal with the problem without telling her the details. She didn't want the dog, but the thought of me turning him loose or taking him to the pound would have disturbed her. Mary Ellen was like this with mice, as well. She wanted to rid the house of pests, but the details of a rodent's demise and how it was disposed of were not to be discussed. Kinda like when people got whacked on *The Sopranos*.

While Mary Ellen and Brett were gone, I scrutinized the entire house for any additional damage. I wasn't sure why I felt so protective of him, but I knew that if I had any hope of keeping this dog, I needed to keep one mess ahead of him.

And did he belong to someone? Had he escaped? Been kicked out of someone's house? I don't know why, but it never dawned on me that someone might be looking for this dog. Quite the contrary. This dog was the one doing the looking. And he had found me.

I also found a few things. The beagle had gotten down in the basement and clawed the drywall all the way through to the insulation. I also discovered he had mangled Brett's treasured Lego collection. I don't think he swallowed any of the pieces, but it was fair to say that none of them fit together anymore. I thought some of this stuff was hilarious. Apparently I was the only one.

No, Mary Ellen was not amused. She was a dog lover, but Barney would be a clear test of her true canine adoration. He seemed nothing like Sabra, the mixed breed we'd acquired just after we got married and moved to Columbus, Ohio. Sabra was what a dog was supposed to be: a joy, not a job. Nor was Barney like Tina, Mary Ellen's dog when she was growing up in Michigan. Tina was a border collie. Barney was borderline crazy. It would be hard for Mary Ellen to make the transition from previous loyal and protective companions to a hyper hound. My wife liked her dogs docile, not demonic. The Wolfsies had wanted a new pet ever since Sabra died, but the plan was that we would select the dog, not the other way around.

Barney remained at home for almost a week while I went to work. It seemed like a year to Mary Ellen. His behavior did not improve. On the second day, I locked him in an empty downstairs bedroom while I was on location for a television shoot. He howled so incessantly that Mary Ellen had to tie him up in the backyard. This was not a dog with a lot of experience being tethered to anything. More howling. Howling for the remainder of the decade and beyond. And this was week one.

"I think he misses you," Mary Ellen told me after several days. "And he loves you." I was being set up. I knew it . . . she knew it . . . hell, the dog knew it. I was unsure what my wife's motive was in this declaration. Clearly, the dog was going to pose a problem if we adopted him, but Mary Ellen was good at reading me—over the years she had become a little too good. She knew the dog and I had the potential for some serious separation anxiety if our relationship had to end. And so Mary Ellen went on the offensive. Her mission was first and foremost homeland security, but I think she also knew it was already too late to break up the relationship between Barney and me. We were soul mates. Mary Ellen thought we had the potential to be cell mates.

For most of the next week, I covered for Barney. Any mischief that occurred during the day, I tried to clean up before Mary Ellen got home, and I attempted, sometimes unsuccessfully, to always keep him within my sight. If I did have to leave the house, I again locked him in that basement bedroom. But after the second day of confinement, he chewed and scratched through the corrugated wood door, creating a ragged porthole he could stick his state of the art nose through.

Mary Ellen tried to be understanding. She really did. But the handwriting was on the wall—what was left of it. "Look, this is real simple, Dick. We have to find the dog a loving home or a minimum-security facility. Either that or you take him to work with you."

She was quite serious. She never actually used the phrase "It's either me or the dog," but implicit in the original options presented was the recognition that the dog needed my supervision 24/7 if he was to stay a member of our household. Oh, yeah: Mary Ellen kept reminding me how much he adored me. She kept bringing that up. She knew exactly what she was doing. She loved it when a plan worked.

She was right, of course. I was head-over-paws crazy about the dog. Yes, he had pain-in-the-ass written all over him, but I knew I could overlook it—the way my elementary school teachers had failed to do with me. Like Barney, I had always been a troublemaker, but most of my teachers never saw through the mischief—and I was judged by the disruption I caused in their lives, not the smiles I was bringing to others. That's the potential I saw in Barney. He might be disruptive, but he could be an impending source of amusement. That dog was me when I was in grade school.

Maybe there was even more to it. A dog is man's best friend, and I was a man who needed a friend. Oh, I knew everybody in Indianapolis and everybody knew me. But my whole existence was about trying to please people, then waiting for their judgment or that of my bosses. I was one of those TV personalities you either found very funny or extremely annoying. I yearned for a companion, but one who wouldn't say, "Boy, the show really stunk today." Or "You are a hoot, Wolfsie." Actually, I wanted somebody who wouldn't say anything.

Oh, and he was a beagle. And a guy. A frou frou French poodle would not have worked. Thanks for not making me explain that.

Yeah, I was hooked. It would be nice to have a furry friend next to me in the car as I drove back and forth to work. I didn't give much thought as to what to do with him during the two hours I was on TV.

I also hoped his behavior would change. But it was my life that changed. And the lives of everyone else Barney touched.

The First Week

I was a feature reporter at WISH-TV, the Indianapolis CBS affiliate, when Barney came into my life. Every morning I reported live from various places around the city, updating the viewers on what was going on in Indy. The problem was that there wasn't that much going on at that time of day, which is why, as you will see, I amended the original job description quite a bit. And my partner-to-be helped me make it happen.

I never intended to introduce a canine superstar to the airwaves. In fact, the first week I took Barney with me, the objective was simply to have a buddy and avoid a divorce. Barney clearly had the potential to cause a broken home. He had already done quite a lot to cause a broken house.

The first couple days, I kept Barney in the car while I hosted the three early morning segments on *Daybreak,* the Channel 8 morning news show. He wasn't happy in the car, even though I kept the motor running with the heat on. He didn't like the confinement, and he made it clear that he wanted to get some air. Little did either of us know that twelve years later, he'd have more airtime than most of the reporters in Indianapolis!

Barney's siren-like howl was so loud that even 100 yards from the broadcasting site, my microphone picked up the bellowing. I didn't mention Barney to the viewers the first few days, figuring he would tire of the yapping and finally mollify his behavior enough that he'd be allowed to remain at home while I was at work. There was no realistic chance of either happening.

The racket was so intense that the station did get a few phone calls from curious—and concerned—viewers who wanted to know why, no matter where I went for my telecast, you could hear this wailing in the background. When the receptionist who screened the calls asked me how to respond to the inquiries, I told her to suggest to people it was a problem with their TV set. In my opinion that was always the best way to explain technical difficulties to the viewers.

I tried parking the car closer to each reporting location so Barney would not feel abandoned, but this had the opposite effect and made him even more determined to get my attention. Now that he could see and hear—and probably smell—me, the volume of his yelping only increased.

Because it was winter, some of the segments were indoors. I was reluctant to request of my guests that Barney be allowed to come into their homes or offices. I knew what had happened to my own home and office. I could leave him in the car, but I knew how unhappy he was alone. In addition, it meant leaving the car turned on so I could leave the heat running. He accidentally figured out that the electric windows lowered if he stepped on the button. And that meant he could scamper out the window, which he did twice in the first few months. Fortunately, in the early days he was reluctant to venture far from me, and I found him sniffing around the area. But he gained confidence quickly and leaving him in the car with the heat or AC on just wasn't viable anymore.

One morning when I sensed his bellowing would wake up the neighborhood, I asked permission to bring him into the senior citizens' home in Mooresville, Indiana, where I was doing a segment. The residents were putting on a talent show and they had no problem with Barney being tied up inside. They did stress the words *tied up*. I borrowed some cord from the center and attached him to a doorknob.

One of the first guests was a spry octogenarian whose talent was doing the hula. She wiggled out from behind the curtain and began doing the native dance. Her grass skirt was seductively flapping about. Not seductive to me, I assure you, but seductive to a year-old beagle that chased and chewed anything that moved.

Barney, securely tied—or so I thought—beagle-eyed the hula dancer's skirt, busted off of his lead, and raced to his intended target. In a flash, he grabbed a hunk of the skirt in his teeth and ripped it off the woman. Completely off.

Fortunately, the woman had worn sufficient undergarments to keep the show rated PG-13, but my cameraman at the time, Marcus Collins, almost broke his neck trying to whip the camera around to feature a more family-friendly picture. He was also laughing so hard, we barely got through the rest of the show.

The residents took it well, considering they hadn't seen anything quite like that at the Mooresville Senior Citizens' Home for some years.

When we left, we were invited back (by all the men).

That was Barney's first appearance on TV. I'm not even sure viewers realized he was my dog. Actually, at that point I wasn't sure, either. My wife had not granted official permission. A few colleagues at the station asked me about the pooch and why he was with me during my segment. I kept it all low-key; after all, he wasn't a hit on the home front and if my bosses ended up feeling the same way as my family, Barney wouldn't have anywhere to go.

Homeland Security

Barney was not winning any popularity contests at the Wolfsies. I dragged him to work with me every day, but he still had to be home the other twenty hours. During that time, I watched him like a hawk, knowing that if I could brag about an unblemished record for even a week, there was a chance that the majority voting bloc in our family would determine a favorable outcome about whether he would achieve squatters' rights in our home. On some level, my wife knew we were going to keep him, but maybe she held hope that even I would soon tire of his shenanigans and find him a good home. There was no chance of that, of course.

At one point, after Barney had successfully unraveled a complete roll of toilet paper that now snaked through the entire house, I sensed the scales were tipping against us. I delivered an ultimatum to the dog in front of my wife, knowing full well that this plea would fall on deaf (but floppy) ears, but I hoped it might sway my wife's growing reluctance to Barney's taking up permanent residence.

"If you keep up this behavior," I said, shaking my finger at him, "I will have to take you to the pound and when you get there you will have to be in a little cage all day and there will be no human food and there's a good chance that if no one adopts you within a couple of weeks, they might have to . . . well, you know . . . put you to sleep."

At first his tail started wagging, which probably meant he thought I was saying, "give you a treat," not "put you to sleep." But then I swear that Barney's eyes shifted to Mary Ellen. "Is he serious?" he wanted to know. I wasn't, of course, but my point did not go unnoticed by my wife. I felt bad about using this threatening approach, but I was hoping to appeal to Mary Ellen's basic love for animals. Not this animal, of course. But animals in general.

Except for that inadvertent emergence on the screen, Barney made only one other television appearance that first week. Part of my routine each morning, other than the three-minute live shots every half hour, were a series of teases— short bits with me promoting my upcoming segment on the news. "Next on *Daybreak,* a munchkin from *The Wizard of Oz.*" You wanted to hook the viewers, keep them watching.

In one interview at a bakery, I walked viewers through the process of making fresh bagels with the manager of the new store. For one of the tease shots for the upcoming segment, I took Barney from the car and stood with him outside the store. When we went live for the tease, I allowed him to lap up the remaining contents of a container of cream cheese. As he happily inhaled the treat, I shamefully said: "Coming up on *Daybreak,* beagles and cream cheese."

Dreadful, I know, and it was just the beginning. We had 6,000 more teases left in our career together.

***

By the end of February, Mary Ellen and I were sleeping in separate rooms on weeknights—not because the romance was cooling, but because my *Daybreak* gig required a 3:30 AM departure from our house. Barney and I had become roommates in the guest room. He would nudge his butt up next to me in anticipation of what he hoped would be a normal night's sleep for a furry carnivore: sixteen straight hours, no problem. *I'll urinate 200 times when I get up tomorrow,* he must have figured.

And so the first few months of this sleeping arrangement created a tricky human-canine conflict: I didn't always want to get up and go to work, but I had to. Barney didn't want to get up and go to work with me because nature had granted him the ability of endless slumber, but he had to. And I had to make him.

It was tough staggering into the downstairs bathroom at 3:30 AM that first winter. I never wore makeup on camera, so that sped up the morning process, but my departure was ultimately slowed because our older home had a detached garage filled with debris left by the previous owner. My car was left out each night, so I had to scrape my windshield on most cold mornings. Barney, knowing he was part of my scheduled exodus, would either retreat under the covers or head upstairs for the master bedroom in expectation of sharing a bed with my wife . . . a hope even *I* had pretty much relinquished Monday through Thursday. One of my favorite lines from *Happy Days* is when Mr. C. makes a romantic gesture to his wife while watching TV one evening. "Oh, Howard," she coos at his touch. "It's only Thursday."

So, morning after morning of that particularly brutal Indiana winter, I dragged two asses out of bed every day— mine and Barney's. I wanted to maintain marital harmony. The weekend was always just around the corner. I might get lucky.

By March, I was sensing that Mary Ellen had softened a little in her antipathy toward Barney and that a conciliatory final gesture might cement the deal. I enrolled Barney in obedience school. As it turned out, Barney was smarter than I was. If I had known how being "bad" would be part of his charm and would add to his success on camera, I might have given this more thought, but at that point I was just eager to win points with my bride.

The woman who took the call at the school was a legend in Indianapolis, running the oldest existing dog training facility in the state. I was impressed with the sales pitch, including the money-back guarantee. She had gone through about half of her spiel when she asked the breed of my pet. When I said beagle, there was dead silence on her end of the phone . . . then a good-natured laugh. "I was just kidding about the guarantee."

She explained that beagles were tough to train but that with dedication and perseverance and $40 an hour, it might be possible to overcome 2,000 years of evolutionary instinct in six hourlong sessions. Darwin must have been rolling over in his grave.

"Oh, and there is homework," she told me. "You are the one responsible for your dog's behavior. We just give you the tools." The tools I needed were an Oreck vacuum cleaner and a backhoe, but I was going to try to make this work.

Those six weeks were the most humiliating of my life. Barney just saw this as a chance to sniff a few . . . well, you get my point.

As mortifying as the experience was, I have always wished that I would have videotaped the final day—graduation, if you will. In the "stay-and-come" test, all the dogs were lined up. It was quite an assortment of talent, too:

big, little, purebreds, mutts, howlers, whiners. Each owner told his or her dog to stay, then turned and walked fifty feet to the back of the training room. Every single one of the dogs stayed right in line—with one notable exception. He certainly never did this when we went for a walk, but for the first time ever, Barney followed me. He actually followed me. Hey, maybe the training was working. Sort of.

Barney was placed back in line. Part two of the final exam was to see if the dogs would go to their owners. Barney had just proven he could do that. Everyone called their dogs. Each dog scampered to his owner. You guessed it, there was one exception . . . again. Barney headed for the kitchen area and launched himself into a trash can containing the remains of someone's beef burrito.

Later that night, all the dogs got a diploma. Including Barney. Like my cousin's online PhD, it meant nothing. Even the Irish setter outperformed Barney.

Some of the owners were bragging about their pets' new behaviors. "Selma wants to be a rescue dog." "Chotsie is going to herd sheep." "Arnold will be a watchdog."

I looked into Barney's big brown eyes. He bowed his head and his ears cascaded over his eyes. Was it shame? "You're going to do just fine," I told him. I was dead-on about that, but at the time, I had some serious doubts.

"How'd it go?" asked Mary Ellen when we walked in the door later that evening.

"I think it was a huge waste of time," I admitted. Mary Ellen gave us both a hug. We needed it.

Obedience school lasted six weeks, but during that time, Barney was making more and more appearances on-screen, including one that was a major factor in his career development, defining what made Barney a TV celebrity.

By late March, the morning anchors half expected that I would somehow work Barney into one of the segments or teases—a cameo appearance, if you will. I tried to balance his play on the air because I had never asked or received permission from either of my bosses to include a dog in my segment. This was either a very gutsy move on my part or monumentally stupid. I knew eventually I'd find out.

Before you read the following story, I'm going to admit something: I'm not sure it's 100 percent true. I've told it for so long that I can't remember anymore. Vince Welsh, then our sports anchor, can't remember either. But we think it's true. Most of it, anyway. That's the way of legends.

When I brought Barney on the show and my segment was outside, I would usually keep him tethered to a stake. (To a dog that doesn't know what a homonym is, this would sound like fun!) To keep him in my view, I often placed him near the portable TV set I used to monitor what was going on back at the station.

After one of Vince's sports updates, he was to toss it to me in the field (a nice sports metaphor). Then Vince, who got a kick out of my bringing the dog on TV, asked about Barney while we were live on the air. I wasn't happy about the inquiry. True, the dog was now appearing on the air more regularly, but anchor recognition of this ongoing event assigned it a new credibility, like it was really part of the show. I wasn't sure how this would play with the bosses.

"Where's Barney?" asked Vince.

"Oh, he's tied up over there by the TV."

Vince couldn't resist: "Well, he must be watching me. I guess he's a big fan."

At that point, Marcus, my photographer, panned to Barney, who had been sniffing around the perimeter of the

TV monitor. Just as the camera zeroed in on him, he lifted his leg and peed right on the twelve-inch Magnavox screen.

"Yeah, Vince, he's a *big* fan."

In television, one way you know you have connected with that invisible audience of viewers is the crew's reaction. In the background, through the anchors' microphones, I could hear the laughter of the cameraman, directors, and producers. Barney had a way of putting a person in his place. Sometimes it was a better place. Vince was an eager and talented new face on our station in those days. Not cocky, really, but self-assured. We can all use a touch of humility.

That moment on TV was graphic enough that it led to a note in my mailbox from general manager, Paul Karpowicz. My worst fears were confirmed. It brought back memories of every note I had ever gotten from a teacher or principal: SEE ME.

A Boy's Life—or, Raised by Wolfsies

"See me" **really did send** chills down my spine. I guess it's because I spent lots of time in the principal's office as a kid in New York. Every report card from kindergarten through sixth grade was one teacher's lament after the other, a verbal wringing of the hands. My parents were told I had no self-control, I was a wise guy, and I was caretaker of the messiest desk in the history of Roosevelt School. I could have been the poster child for ADD. But they had not invented that diagnosis yet.

For me there was quite literally no prescription for success. Every day was torture, sitting for hours listening to the teacher, desperately searching for the right time to offer a wisecrack to the class. There was the one thing I was good at: ad-libbing. I even remember my first real gem back in the third grade. Miss Davis had cautioned a student about the danger of chewing on his pencil.

"What would happen if you swallowed that pencil?" she asked Mark Fisher.

My hand shot up. "He could borrow my pen."

The crowd went wild. But I was in trouble, as always. I sat for two hours after class and had the privilege of writing my little wisecrack 1,000 times on the blackboard. Comedy is hard work.

Then came junior high school. I don't remember a thing about junior high. My sense is that that is a good thing.

I do remember Pokie, my first dog and I guess my first real experience loving an animal. We had gotten the black and white speckled mixed breed from the Humane Society to appease my sister Linda, who was so obsessed with dogs at age six that when she got out of the bathtub, she would shake like a pooch caught in a downpour. A canine companion was a cheaper route than long-term therapy, so the Wolfsies got a dog.

Just months after Pokie arrived, she escaped from the house. I chased her to the end of our block, just in time to see a car crash into her back legs as she crossed the main thoroughfare. Pokie yelped and limped home. It was traumatizing to see this, but the injury was not as bad as we had thought, although her tail had been completely crushed and required amputation.

My mother, who I am not sure had truly bonded with the dog at the time, became her dedicated health care provider for the next ten years. The remaining stump lacked mobility, which meant my mother had to clean Pokie each day when she returned from her daily constitutional—but not before Pokie had soiled clothing and furniture. Mom loved that dog. Her dedication to that needy pup showed me what dedication to an animal meant.

In school, I was seldom a serious pupil, often a dedicated punster and the runaway favorite for class clown my senior year. I got a 35 in the state Regents Test in chemistry. That's out of 100. But on my English regents, I scored 40 out of 40 on the written exam, a surprise even to me because my 300-word essay was filled with corny plays on words and sentence fragments. Which I still like to use.

New Rochelle High School was just like a big stage for me, an audience that would laugh at almost anything if I had the nerve to blurt it out in class during a lesson on *The Scarlet Letter*. Occasionally, I'd even get a grin from a teacher, which is really the highest compliment. When I became a teacher several years later, I remembered how much that reaction had meant to me and I consciously doled out chuckles and smiles to deserving students who managed a clever ad-lib in class.

In August 1965, my parents dropped me on the corner of 21st and I Street in the nation's capital, just a few blocks from the White House. I had never been away from my parents. I didn't know a soul in this new city. I was homesick for my family and friends.

And I was going to miss my audience.

Getting laughs turned out be a lot easier than getting laid, evidenced by the fact that I graduated from college at the peak of the sexual revolution with zero experience in pleasing a woman, but rave reviews when it came to performing for a crowd.

Freshman year I began slipping anonymous essays under the door of the newspaper editor, a technique that apparently both Ben Franklin and Mark Twain had used to get their first break in publishing. By sophomore year I had fessed up to my ploy after a few of my essays were printed, and soon I began writing a weekly humor column for the school paper, *The Hatchet*.

By my junior year, my chutzpah had kicked in again and I had orchestrated a way to distribute my column in one hundred college newspapers, becoming the first student syndicated humor column in history—as far as I knew. Incredibly, checks kept appearing in my mailbox at the dorm, payment for the right to use my material. It was the closest I ever got to getting high. And this was the sixties.

As it happened, the man who had inspired me to pursue a humor column of my own lived right here in Washington. And ever since I'd begun college, I had wanted to meet him, the number-one syndicated writer in the country: Art Buchwald. So I finally got up my courage and looked up his home number in the phone book—not that he would be listed. But there it was.

Incredibly, Mr. Buchwald answered his home phone. I told him I was a fan. That I wrote a humor column, just like his. Yeah, right. Silence on the other end. I also informed him that I attended the university just a few blocks from where he worked. "Call my office," he said. "Let's see just how funny you are." It was like an Old West gunfighter throwing down a challenge.

A week later, I entered Buchwald's office with a stack of *Hatchets* under my arm. He put both feet up on his desk. Not one at a time; instead, he propelled both of his hefty legs together onto the mahogany surface with a thud. There was a hole in one of his shoes.

Buchwald stole a glance at me and snapped, "Let me see one of those newspapers, kid." He ripped open the current issue and began reading my column. I watched his face. Nothing. He grabbed a pen off his desk and scribbled a few words over my byline. He apologized that something had come up. With that, he left. The entire meeting with him lasted but ten minutes.

Dejected, I shuffled along Pennsylvania Avenue back to my apartment, but I stopped at the first corner bench and opened *The Hatchet* to the page that Buchwald had read just minutes before. I stared in delight at these words scrawled on the page: "Wolfsie, stay out of my racket."—Art Buchwald. To this day, I assume he meant he saw me as a potential competitor, but I suppose at the time it could have been just good advice for someone with no talent who needed to pursue a more realistic line of work.

In 1969 I graduated from the George Washington University, and with diploma in hand, I headed home. That May, only a war in Vietnam stood between me and the rest of my life. I did oppose the war, but the truth was that even if I had embraced the politics of the conflict, the idea of shooting a gun and killing anyone was unthinkable. Being shot *at*, I wasn't good at thinking about either. Knock 'em dead with jokes was my way of dealing with people. "Stop, you're killing me" was the refrain I looked forward to hearing someday in a comedy club in New York. Not in Vietnam.

What *do* you do with a degree in American Studies? I knew I was creative and a fairly good writer. Maybe advertising? But writing spots for Pepsodent on Madison Avenue was not going to keep me out of the draft.

Teaching had always intrigued me, although I had this unrealistic notion that to teach something, you had to know something. Despite my four years of post–high school education, I didn't think I'd feel any more confident in a classroom than in a rice paddy. When I learned that teaching positions were open at my alma mater, New Rochelle High School, I decided it was worth a try.

When I called to make an appointment at the central office, the secretary said the superintendent of schools wanted to know if I was the same Dick Wolfsie who had gone to New Rochelle High just four years earlier. Stupidly, I told the truth, and I'll never forget her retort: "Dr. Misner said to come in anyway."

I did get the job, but the department chairwoman who hired me had a clear memory of my senior year, just five years earlier. She had also taught my mother, apparently another poor student, she kindly shared with me." This is the worst hiring I have ever made," she told me, wagging her finger. Fact is, she was desperate. School began in a few weeks.

Faculty members who had disciplined me for my antics, teachers who had rolled their eyes at my one-liners and admonished my parents about my lack of appropriate reserve, were now my colleagues. For nine years, I taught psychology. Then English, as well. Teaching psychology allowed for more innovation and demonstration in the class. When I blind-folded students and had them run through a maze of chairs, the chair of the department heard about my technique and informed me that I could have just as easily taught the concept through lecture, not a demo that caused a great deal of disruption in the room. She was wrong, of course. I knew how to work an audience.

The teachers and the students nicknamed me Kotter, a reference to the TV show *Welcome Back, Kotter,* where Gabe Kaplan in the title role returns to teach at his alma mater. I was also dubbed "rookie of the year" by the more experienced teachers. I instinctively knew how to inform and entertain at the same time, the one-two punch for effective teaching and hosting of a talk show. But the latter was still a decade away.

The summer of '78 looked like it would be typical, chasing girls and golf balls, but a call from a friend would soon mean the beginning of a roller-coaster series of events that took me from a high school psychology teacher to the host of the number-one local morning show in the country in only two years.

The call was from Burt Dubrow, a high school buddy, whose obsession with TV had resulted in a myriad of media jobs since college, including emceeing and producing a revival of the legendary *Howdy Doody Show* on college campuses. Burt was producing a series of shows for Warner Cable in Columbus, Ohio. Viewers had their homes hardwired so they could interact via a tiny box, not unlike a TV remote. Based on questions elicited from the game- and talk-show hosts, viewers could register opinions and provide feedback, which then appeared on the screen fully tabulated. It was so advanced for its time that Phil Donahue did a show from one of the studios, heralding the new technology.

I became a writer and associate producer for the evening talk show as well as a weekend kids' program. I moved from New York to Columbus, Ohio, to start a new life. I watched the host of the evening program each night read my questions verbatim and knew that I could do it better and more spontaneously. How did I know that? Because for a decade I had managed to keep the attention of thirty hormone-charged adolescents for forty minutes five times a day with a technique that combined just the right mixture of information and entertainment. That's exactly what a good talk-show host does. But how would I get a job like that? Not a clue.

In the early fall, Burt's wife introduced me to one of her friends, a stunning redhead who was not looking for a husband but was seeking an MBA at the University of Michigan. Mary Ellen drove from Ann Arbor to Columbus for the blind date and we had dinner at Burt's home.

Mary Ellen and I were total opposites by any observable criteria. She was measured and reserved. She actually let people finish sentences when they were speaking. This really threw me because in New York the only way you know you are done talking is when someone interrupts you. Initially, she was put off by the interaction between Burt and me, which often bordered on the juvenile as we relived our childhood together and fell into fits of laughter during the meal.

But in the three days that followed, Mary Ellen and I had more time to talk one-on-one. Despite the obvious differences in demeanor and style, we shared some common values. It was love at fourth sight.

The romance blossomed quickly, maybe too quickly for Mary Ellen, who was interviewing for jobs all over the country and was reluctant to commit to a relationship with a guy who wrote cue cards for a living. When she secured a consulting job in Chicago, we decided to move to the Windy City together, and I would look for freelance work as a writer there.

Before we left for Chicago, on several occasions I had filled in for the evening host, who eventually left the show for the business world. The bosses liked my style and for almost a year, they flew me in from Chicago on Sunday nights, then jetted me home on Wednesdays. I was hosting the show three nights a week.

I don't recall exactly why QUBE took a chance with me, but I think that, like my teaching job, I was the beneficiary of being at the right place at the right time . . . when the people in charge were desperate.

Columbus Alive reached only a small audience, but because the technology was unique, so state of the art, it was not uncommon for reporters from all over the world to be in the control room watching the show. I became a master at what was called a PQ, also known as an interactive question. "Do you think gays should be allowed to teach school?" I asked the audience during a related debate. Then I would proclaim: "touch now," which meant the home viewer could push the appropriate button and register his opinion. Once, during a particularly boring interview, I polled the audience, asking if it was time to excuse my guest and go on to the next portion of the show. The viewers voted. The guest was soon history. And I made a little history. Had something like this ever happened before on a television show? I'm sure not.

One of my first guests on the evening show was Jack Hanna, director of the Columbus Zoo and now a regular with Larry King and David Letterman. So nervous was Hanna on his first TV interview that when I asked him whether the snake he had wrapped around my neck was poisonous, he just stared at me blankly. During the pause, my eyes widened in mock fear. Timing is everything. The crew broke into laughter. I told Jack after the show, "That's a funny bit. Just pretend you're not really that informed about the animals . . . be a little surprised by what they do." Almost thirty years later, Jack is still doing that very act. Is Jack pretending he's clueless or is he acting? You're never sure. That's what makes Jack Hanna so much fun to watch.

The show was like my classroom. There was no live audience, but I often imagined there was a roomful of kids in front of me. It worked. In fact, it worked so well, I became the first cable talk-show host to win a regional Emmy.

We wanted kids, but not quite yet. How about a dog? Enter Sabra, a terrier mix from the Humane Society. She was our first dog together and soon became the central focus in our lives.

Sabra must have always wanted to be a mother because after being spayed, she would steal socks out of our laundry hamper, distribute them on the floor, and guard them as if they were her puppies. If we approached her, she snarled. Socks only a mother could love.

Sabra did fill a void in our lives. We were past twenty-somethings, but an immediate plunge into parenthood did not seem advised given the uncertainty of the TV business. Caring for a dog might give us a little confidence that we could be good "parents," or at least provide some comfort we could move on to the next level of parenting.

In 1980, I received an Emmy Award for Best Talk Show Host in a three-state region of the Midwest. This was the first time in history that the prize had gone to a cable host, as opposed to someone in traditional broadcast TV.

Within weeks, a Boston network affiliate offered me a job as a late-night host, moving me from the tiny Columbus market to the number-five station in the country. While Mary Ellen was off to Bean City searching for an apartment, another call from Burt. "Dick, WABC in New York just called me. They want you to audition for their morning show."

This program, along with its counterpart in L.A., was the number-one local morning show in the country. As a New Yorker, I knew the time slot had a history of turnover after the exit of host Stanley Siegel, a certified neurotic who had left television, probably for long-term therapy. He was a therapist himself, so he probably spent the next few years just talking to . . . well, himself.

Dozens of hosts from around the country had tried out for the gig. But the spot was still vacant.

Incredibly, I was not the least bit nervous during the live on-air audition. I had a firm job offer in Boston, and I was getting the hang of this talk-show thing. And what did I have to lose?

My first guest that morning, a flamboyant fashion designer from Manhattan, was demonstrating the proper beachwear for the summer. He placed a huge sombrero on his own head and said, "No sun will ever touch me." I did a take to the audience, then: "No son of mine, I'll tell you that." Laughter and applause from the spectators and crew. But it was better than that. My mother loved it, too.

The next day I was offered the job on *Good Morning, New York*. My salary was five times what I made in Columbus. But something didn't seem right. And for the next six months nothing was right. My career in the Big Apple was brief, less than a year. Big stars like Woody Allen, Mickey Rooney, James Mason, and Louis Armstrong sat across from me promoting their books and movies. But overall, it was a painful experience. Lots of politics and backstabbing. And not the TV market where they give you much time to *grow* into the job.

Memories of those years have faded, but there were two people I met who I will never forget. They, along with Art Buchwald, shaped my developing sense of how to connect with people. And how to make them laugh.

I had watched Steve Allen on TV in the '50s. When my parents were glued to CBS at 8 PM on Sunday nights watching Ed Sullivan, I took the hipper option and retreated to the basement to watch Steve Allen on ABC. Steve was *The Tonight Show*'s first host and the inventor of late-night TV talk shows. Many of the routines we are so familiar with today, from Johnny Carson's Carnac to Jay Leno's man-on-the-street interviews, were Steve Allen's creations.

Steve would smear his body with dog food and unleash a pack of assorted dogs. He strapped a kite to his back and ran into a huge fan. Mr. Allen put a live camera on the corner of Hollywood and Vine and commented on the people who walked by. Sound familiar? Carson, Letterman, and Leno have all copied it in one form or another.

I first met Mr. Allen during an interview on *Good Morning, New York*. We were talking about the great comic actor Stan Laurel. "Where can you find people of that ilk anymore?" asked Mr. Allen. "You could join the Ilks Club," I said. It was a Steve Allen kind of joke. And we both knew it. He laughed. Yes, I had made Steve Allen laugh.

If there was anyone sillier than Steve Allen, it was Soupy Sales. As a twelve-year-old, I was glued to the TV while Soupy sparred with his off-camera puppet friends: White Fang, "the meanest dog in the U.S.A.," and Black Tooth, "the sweetest dog in the world." Only the paws of these puppets were shown, and White Fang did little more than grunt. Soupy would then translate the incomprehensible sounds. I had the opportunity to work with Soupy Sales for a week while at WABC. It almost made the gig worthwhile. Almost.

Six months after I started in New York, I was done. My cohost didn't like me. The producer didn't like my style. The general manager, I discovered, didn't know who the hell I was. He had been in Europe when his station manager hired me. I knew things had been too easy. I was toast. The meeting with the station manager was short and ugly. "I'm afraid you're not quite what we are looking for, but we wish you the best of luck."

All of a sudden that $1,100-a-month apartment on Third Avenue didn't seem like such a good deal. I spent Tuesdays in the unemployment line, often signing autographs for people who thought I was doing some kind of news story. I tried to find freelance work doing commercials, but I was so bad at it that I auditioned to play a talk-show host in a beer ad, and I wasn't even good enough for a second audition.

Mary Ellen had a good job as a marketing director at one of the local hospitals. The first six weeks, we lived in the

Essex House near Central Park until we found an apartment. Everything was courtesy of WABC, including meals. A dream come true. My wife compared herself to Eloise, the little girl in Kay Thompson's 1950s children's book, who lived at the Plaza Hotel and endlessly roamed the hotel in search of adventure. Why not take it easy for a while and enjoy the Big Apple? We had not anticipated how rotten things would get.

Mary Ellen and I moved back home to my mother and father's house in New Rochelle, just a mile from New Rochelle High School, where I once held the world's most secure job. I bartended for a few months and Mary Ellen, America's best-looking MBA, took part-time work as a Kelly Girl temp at six bucks an hour. Two months earlier I had been picked up in a limo to get to work. Now I had no idea what we were going to do. I was thirty-five years old, newly married, and living at home with Mom and Dad.

After I left WABC, another entourage of hapless hosts tried to make the cut, rarely lasting more than a few weeks. Within a year, WABC finally hired my permanent replacement, a guy named Regis Philbin, who was then in L.A. doing a similar show. People tell me he's done okay.

In August of '81, I responded to an ad in *Broadcasting Magazine*. The local CBS affiliate in Indianapolis needed male and female hosts for a new show. At the time, Indy was more the butt of jokes than a mecca for media, but I was in no position to be choosy.

For the audition, I had been paired by pure chance with a midwestern gal who had been on the radio in Dayton, Ohio. Patty Spitler was a feisty, quick-witted blonde. The chemistry between us was evident to everyone. The next day the general manager called the two of us into his office and offered us the job. Then this:

"Dick, this may be the dumbest decision I have ever made."

I had heard this before. That was the kind of insightful thinking that had gotten me my high school teaching job.

"Our viewers will not like you at first. You're too New York. This is Indiana. But the show needs an edge. I think you will grow on people." Nice—he made me sound like some kind of fungus. But at least I had a job. Like most mushrooms, I lasted little more than a season.

In a cost-cutting move, *Indianapolis Afternoon* was dumped. Now I had been canned twice in two years. When most TV personalities lose a job they split to another TV market. You look like damaged goods. But Mary Ellen had a good job. As for me? Writing, teaching, bartending? Something would come up . . . wouldn't it?

WPDS was a new independent station. Maybe there was something there. I marched myself over there after managing to wrangle a meeting with the GM, whom I convinced to let me create a late-night show, not unlike the one I had been offered in Boston, to feature what I called fringe people, locals who didn't usually get much air time because of their out-of the-mainstream lifestyle and beliefs.

It was quite a ride for over a year. I interviewed Holocaust deniers, professional wrestlers, and the KKK. Pornographers, transsexuals, transvestites, gay teens, prostitutes, they all appeared on *Night Talk*. But the show aired only once a week. Lots of mayhem. No money.

It was time for action. The $10 million project to refurbish the old downtown Indianapolis Union Station as a festival marketplace was about six months from completion. I looked at the building and realized it would be a perfect place for a morning TV show, something Indy had not had in several years. Something I hadn't had in a few years myself.

Using a little New York chutzpah, I managed to convince both the local TV affiliate and the Union Station developer that the idea had merit. Incredibly, they agreed. I would be host and producer of this morning TV show.

AM Indiana held its own for almost five years—quite a long run in the talk business. But it was a bad time to be in the talk business on a local station. After five years, the combined competition of Oprah and Phil Donahue, airing at the same time on different stations, buried us. I ended up with more awards than viewers. Out of work again. I was getting good at this—losing my job, that is.

What was I doing wrong? Why did every TV position I ever had start with a bang and end with a whimper? I didn't know it then, but my career breakthrough was six months away. This time it would *begin* with a whimper.

So You Think This Is Funny?

There were only two kinds of meetings I had ever had with a general manager: the kind where I got the job and the kind where I lost one. So it will come as no surprise that I was a bit nervous when I was called into General Manager Paul Karpowicz's office. I didn't bring Barney with me, although Paul was such a nice guy that I thought it would have been hard for him to look into the beagle's deep brown eyes and tell him his career was over already. Of course, I had a fair amount of experience in this area, so I prepared for the worst.

"Sit down, Dick." *Always a bad sign,* I thought. "Did you think that was funny the way the dog urinated on the TV monitor?" he asked sternly.

Paul's question was an awfully good one. I did think it was funny . . . but did he? He didn't ask me if I thought he thought it was funny. He asked me what I thought was funny. Now I was so flustered I opted for something against my better judgment: the truth.

"Paul, I thought it was the funniest thing I've ever seen." I held my breath.

"So did I, Wolfsie, so did I. The dog will be a great addition to the morning news."

"Even though he peed on a TV in front of all our viewers?"

"If the ratings go up, he can take a dump in my office."

Two weeks later, that's exactly what Barney did—right next to Paul's prized ficus plant, after a station meeting.

At that point, Barney and I were on Paul's good list. But it hadn't always been that way. When I was originally hired as the morning reporter, it was, I later discovered, not without some clear reservations on his part. My short list of potential news stories had included segments on how the corned beef was delivered each morning to Shapiro's, the local eatery that had a reputation for being as close to New York (and heaven) as any delicatessen in Indiana. I also included a possible segment where I would sit in on a conversation with a small group of Jewish men, including several Holocaust survivors, who for thirty years had huddled at the deli every morning at 6 AM to kibbitz about the world while they gobbled lox and bagels. Oh, and it would be cool to show how they make bagels. Oy, what a mistake.

When Karpowicz saw the list, he told news director Lee Giles that he was concerned that I was obsessed with Jewish things. He wondered if I would be able to expand my horizons and find other kinds of segments. He had a point. The Jewish population was not exactly a big demographic in Indiana. I submitted a new list that was more ecumenical, and I ultimately got the job. And, with Barney and a little luck, I would keep it.

Months after that incident in Paul's office, Barney had what you might call an encore performance. I did a *Daybreak* segment just outside the PR firm Caldwell Van Riper on Meridian Street in Indianapolis. We were highlighting a sports mural that had been painted on the side of their building, showcasing the Indiana Pacers.

Right next door to Caldwell Van Riper is WRTV Channel 6, the ABC affiliate, one of Channel 8's rival stations. Normally, I'd do everything possible to prevent their sign and logo from being seen on our program. But as the live shoot began, I noticed that Barney had roamed away from me and was sniffing along the grounds of the Channel 6 property.

What I saw next required an immediate journalistic decision, a judgment call that put into play all of my experience as a broadcast professional. Should I tell Carl Finchum, my new photographer, to pan over to the Channel 6 lawn and get a shot of Barney? Sure. Why not? "Carl," I said on camera, "show the viewers what Barney thinks of the competition."

The camera panned . . . and . . . you guessed it: tens of thousands of loyal Channel 8 viewers watched as my lovable beagle squatted next to the Channel 6 sign and left a substantial reminder of his visit. Man, talk about product placement!

"How'd you get him to do that?" people asked me the next day.

"We've been practicing for weeks," I said.

And I think some people believed me.

A Dog's Life

The meeting with Paul was definitely positive. He loved the dog and wanted him to remain part of the morning news block. More important, he wanted *me* to remain part of the morning news block. The downside was that he, like so many others, believed that when the dog did something funny, I had somehow orchestrated it. At the end of the meeting, he even said to me, "The peeing on the monitor was funny. But it won't be funny the second time." Was he serious? The dog had a mind of his own and minding me was not part of the game plan. I couldn't say, "Okay, be funny." I couldn't even do that with myself.

And there was another element: I was accustomed to being the center of attention. The emphasis was shifting. Was the tail wagging the hog? Was this my first tinge of Barney jealousy? Was I envious of a stray hound with absolutely no previous TV experience?

I spent several days mulling this over. Finally I decided I was looking at this the wrong way. What other TV reporter had a dog as a sidekick? This human/canine team could be a meal ticket to success for both of us.

What we needed, though, was a breakthrough moment, a segment that people would talk about around the water cooler. All the promotion you can buy, all the billboards, all the print ads pale in comparison to word of mouth. The next week a gift arrived from heaven in the form of a letter, a gift that kept on giving for the next eleven years, and it became the most repeated show, kicking off every highlight tape of Barney's many years on TV.

While most viewers were enjoying Barney's mischief, one viewer was troubled by the shenanigans—or at least thought that *I* was. On air, I continually lamented the dog's destructive behavior, playing the victim's role, and pretending that his behavior was more than I could handle, which was certainly true at home. So distressed did I appear that Dr. Gary Sampson, a former research veterinarian with Eli Lilly, wrote me a sympathetic note claiming he could be of assistance. Sampson had retired from Lilly and had started a new career dealing exclusively with dog and cat behavior. I read the letter and immediately called him.

"I can help Barney with that digging," he told me over the phone.

"Geez, Doc, the last thing Barney needs is help. I want someone to stop him."

Honestly, I didn't want Dr. Sampson's help. Barney's uncontrollable behavior on TV was getting lots of street talk. Hmmm . . . I asked Dr. Sampson to come on the show live and discuss how to remedy the situation. He was hesitant. His practice was primarily done over the phone, and the idea of live TV was frightening and unpredictable to him.

I was good at convincing people to appear on TV (a friend used to say I could talk a dog off a meat truck) and besides, this was good PR for the doctor's new career. So, two weeks later, bright and early, Dr. Sampson and I sat on my front step at 5 in the morning while he pontificated about the animal instinct to dig and chew and some of the possible remedies for besieged dog owners like myself. Barney was unimpressed. He sat there and bayed during the early segments. Neighbors peeped out of doors and windows to see what was causing the disturbance. But as you will now see, it was a day that lived in infamy.

Never in the history of live television has a dog taken a cue better than Barney. At the first mention of digging by Dr. Sampson, Barney was on a mission. His first target was my wife's rosebush near the front stoop. The barrage of dirt was so great that both the doc and I spent most of the interview brushing off the remains of his excavation. Mud and topsoil came spewing from between Barney's legs. Mary Ellen's rose-bush had been deflowered and uprooted. The front porch was a disaster area.

Looking at the pile of dirt that had accumulated at his feet and peering at Barney as he continued to burrow, the good doctor observed: "There must be something down there that he wants."

Ya think?

Dr. Sampson was absolutely right. Actually, I was going to make a similar, albeit layman's assessment of the situation. The dirt kept coming. Barney didn't even let up during the first commercial break. This was always the thing that distinguished him from other television talent. He was no media phony. He was the same on the air and off.

During the break, I mentioned to the doctor that we should probably move from discussing the digging problem to Barney's chewing problem. The vet agreed that was a good idea.

We never did do that segment. As we chatted, Barney chewed through the audio cord from the camera, and so we were off the air. The segment ended. Dave Barras, the anchor back at the station, said we had technical difficulties. Technically, we did. His name was Barney. If YouTube had existed then, we'd have been the number-one download.

Dr. Sampson's career did not suffer from his TV interaction with Barney. In fact, he is today a leading expert on dog and cat behavior. Dr. Sampson seldom meets with the dogs in person; he simply helps the owners correct their ways, consulting over the phone. It is rare for Dr. Sampson to make a house call. Gee, I wonder if he had a bad experience at someone's house.

Dr. Sampson and I lost touch for quite a while, although he apparently followed Barney's career on TV for years. The last thing I wanted was a well-behaved dog and the last thing Dr. Sampson needed was an unmotivated owner. We each had our roles to play. That was contrary to Dr. Sampson's mission, but he understood the situation.

Barney generated a lot of talk at the station and more than a few people stopped me in the grocery store and asked if my new dog had found a full-time job. Now that Barney was appearing almost every day, he was greasing the viewers' early morning routine of getting up and going to work. But I still had no sense if the public had fully come to see us as a team.

Then one evening, the family attended an Indianapolis Indians game at Bush Stadium, the Triple A ballpark downtown. I was trying to encourage Brett to have a little interest in local sports and a night at the ballpark was fun even if you weren't a big baseball fan.

At one point in the game, I retreated to the john and picked up a beer on the way back. As I edged my way through my aisle, I suddenly heard a group of guys who clearly had already downed a few Bud Lights themselves begin a chant: BAR-NEY ... BAR-NEY ... BAR-NEY! Then they bellowed each letter in the name.

They almost spelled it correctly. These were serious fans.

My wife heard the chant and was impressed. "Wow, it's too bad no one can spell *Wolfsie*," she said. But I knew we had arrived. It's amazing the lessons baseball can teach you.

Photo Ops

In my first ten years of television, prior to meeting Barney, I'm guessing that I signed maybe 100 photos of myself for fans. Most of these after a subtle suggestion: "Say, would you like a photo of me? Please?" But when Barney became my partner, I signed thousands.

Most on-air reporters have what is called an eight-by-ten glossy, usually a black-and-white head shot that they use to grant requests from viewers for pictures and autographs. Unless you're a hot female meteorologist, most of us never use up the five hundred photos we are initially given (they are cheaper by the forty dozen). The poor quality of a mass-produced likeness initially made you look ten years older. But it would ultimately make you look ten years younger because the station wouldn't replace them until you gave away the first five hundred. Which was never. I had about 475 left when I first teamed with up Barney. Then no one wanted a photo of *just* me, so I trashed them.

Barney's first photos were courtesy of Ed Bowers of Tower Studio. Ed was an icon in central Indiana and had been taking high school graduation pictures for at least three decades. There was a pretty good chance that if you went to public school in Indianapolis, Ed had taken your yearbook picture. And if you were under thirty there was a better chance he took your mother and father's pictures, as well.

He was also an early-morning TV fan and had been watching Barney emerge as a rising star. Ed wanted to do a full studio shoot with Barney—dozens of poses, different angles, sexy lighting, the works.

Ed was no dummy. Even with all the chemicals you inhaled developing photos in those days, he was clearheaded enough to know he wanted the photo shoot on TV as part of the morning news.

"But, Ed," I pleaded, "it will be chaos. Barney won't sit still; the result will be total pandemonium."

"I know," he said. "And people will talk about it forever."

Then he shot me a cheesy grin, the kind he was so adept at getting from high school seniors. Ed knew the value of good PR.

The morning of the show I was not surprised to see the thought and preparation Ed put into the photo shoot. Ed had lugged in scenery and a small crew of assistants. He brought dog food and treats and a high-pitched whistle to get Barney's attention. He even had a long ladder so he could shoot from above. Why? I had no idea. But I was impressed. At the time, quite frankly, I cared less about the quality of the photos than the fact that this was going to be a great show. I really couldn't lose. Barney would probably dart around the studio, unwilling to sit for even a second, leaving poor Ed actually missing his decades of interaction with adolescents. If that's possible.

The other possibility was that Barney would simply bask in the glow of the moment, lapping up every second of the spotlight, loving being the center of attention. He would be the perfect model. It would be one extreme or the other.

There never was a middle ground. Not with Barney. And it never mattered. It was funny either way.

Barney opted for chaos. Every prop, every play toy, every wastebasket, every treat became a diversion. The few times we managed to get him settled, Ed decided it was a good time to shoot from the ladder, which required about thirty more seconds of waiting time while Ed, who was no spring chicken, managed to slowly—very slowly—hobble his way up the creaky steps. When he finally reached the top, he carefully twisted himself around and then seemed genuinely surprised—and mildly miffed—that Barney had not remained in the spot Ed had assigned to him. Much of this dance was seen on TV. The whole thing seemed choreographed like a Laurel and Hardy routine.

In the final on-air segment, Ed pulled out the heavy hardware. Not a new camera or fancy lens, but an artificial smoke–producing machine, the kind you might use in a movie to create a creepy scene or a steamy, sexy one. "This will make for some very artsy shots," said Ed, beaming.

With Barney finally sitting in a big, comfy recliner, relaxed at last, Ed cranked up the machine and smoke spewed out of the device and into his studio. It also made an odd screeching sound. Ed wasn't real hip on how to use the contraption. Apparently, he didn't get a lot of calls for smoke when he photographed the high school football players.

Never, never had I witnessed my dog, or any dog for that matter, so terrified. His ears virtually shot straight up on the top of his head, his eyes widened like Frisbees, his hair stood on end.

It was funny television, yes, but it was a classic example of that fine line I would sometimes cross where viewers were no longer amused with Barney's antics but concerned about how he was being handled or mishandled. I knew as I watched this fiasco unfold that the station would get dozens of calls with concerns that I had allowed Barney to be harmed. Everyone was beginning to feel they had a vested interest in Barney. "No one is going to mistreat my dog" was the collective feeling.

I spent most of the afternoon later that day on the phone, allaying people's fears. The next morning I opened up the show with Barney at my side, assuring the viewers their favorite news hound was okay and that I swore I would never let something like that happen again. But throughout the years, I was amazed how carefully people scrutinized my interactions with Barney. If I picked him up, I had to be sure to lower him slowly to the ground. If it appeared I "dropped" him (which a certain camera angle might suggest) the station would get calls. If I yelled at him, people chastised me. This was all evidence he was the viewers' dog.

With all the mayhem, we did get a photo that became a classic. The one prop I had brought with me to Tower Studio was Barney's obedience school diploma. The fact that Ed had done so many high school graduations prompted the idea, and I figured that Barney was just as undeserving of a diploma as some eighteen-year-olds, so . . . why not?

Ed put Barney in a chair behind his desk and I propped his paws up on the flat surface, inserting the folded diploma under his paws. Barney seemed content to remain in that position. Ed inched toward the ladder. "I'll break your arm if you climb that ladder," I said. "Just shoot the damn picture."

That photo of Barney was such a favorite that over the years I printed 5,000 of them. I must have signed 4,999 because I have only one left. The only reason I updated the photo was that when Barney began to mature, I thought he deserved a picture that reflected his years of experience. In addition, I decided finally to be in the picture with him. I was, after all, part of the team.

Over the years, I signed each photo the identical way. The person's name came first, then: *Your pals, Dick and Barney.* I tried two different approaches with Barney's signature. One disaster was pressing Barney's paw down on an inkpad. The fans loved it. My wife? Not so much. There were Barney tracks all over the house: another brilliant move on my part to endear my wife to Barney. But at least we knew where he was. Or had been.

I also bought a rubber stamp with a paw print on it. People complained it was too impersonal. The most successful operation involved me drawing his paw, essentially four amoeba shapes half surrounding a small circle. Then I blackened in the outlines with a black magic marker. People did seem genuinely satisfied when I signed for Barney, so that's the way it was for most of the dozen years. I signed for both of us. Barney never lifted a paw to help. No problem.

To this day, when people come up to me to talk about Barney, they inevitably say, "I still have Barney's photo and autograph on my refrigerator."

If they look carefully, they may have mine, too.

***

The incident at Bush Stadium when the fans howled for Barney was substantial proof that he was catching on. It was clear that the anchors and reporters were getting a kick out of the idea of a nonhuman colleague, but I had to be careful. Egos are big. And fragile. None more fragile than mine. From that initial conversation with Paul Karpowicz, I was pleased that he had signed on to the idea, and so had Lee Giles, the news director. From the beginning, they both knew the dog was good for ratings.

"I thought it was great," Paul recalled. "At the time, we were not number one, and we were trying to establish a local identity. Not that we were this smart, but it turned out we were groundbreaking."

"Little by little, it just kind of grew," said Lee. "Barney the dog turned out, over time, to be a very interesting personality. A real dickens around the studio, but viewers just fell in love with him."

I thought it was important for the morning news team to know that the big tunas were onboard. How could I engineer some public display of the GM's acceptance of a dog on the news?

How could I lobby for their open support? Ah, the lobby!

The lobby of WISH-TV was nothing fancy—a kind of '50s retro look with a TV monitor and a coffee table stacked with magazines so guests and clients could bide time while waiting to be summoned by the producers downstairs or the sales reps upstairs. Guests often peered at the framed photos that hung on the south wall. Each color picture was a bigger-than-life-size portrait of our news anchors, representing all of our several daily newscasts, about a dozen or so photos in all.

Now that Barney had his own photos, I wondered whether, just hypothetically, the big shots would consider placing Barney's likeness on that wall. That would mean that someone else's mug would have to be removed to make room.

And so an idea was born. I'd report live from the lobby one morning and take down our star news anchor Dave Barras's photo, then replace it with Barney's. I used one of the photos that Ed Bowers had taken months earlier and had it blown up to the appropriate size.

This is what I call a 6-Up idea. *Almost* perfect, but something was missing. To make it work, I had to legitimize the switch. I needed the transfer made live on TV—by the execs.

This was a charade, of course, but one that would be good for a few laughs and serve my purpose, as well. It also meant getting Paul Karpowicz and Lee Giles up at 4 in the morning to be part of the first segment at 5 AM I wasn't really going to ask them to do this . . . was I?

What the hell. First I asked Giles, who just shook his head and rolled his eyes, but he finally agreed to do it. Then I told him I wanted Karpowicz to do it with him.

"Are you crazy? He's not going to do that."

"Are you sure, Lee? I didn't think you were going to do it, either."

I met with Paul the next day, laid out the plan, and waited for his reaction. "That's damn funny," he said. "Sure. Why not?"

And so it was. We did four segments live, the first in the GM's office at 5:20 AM where I pretended to have a hidden camera listening in on this big executive decision to move Dave Barras's photo off the lobby wall and substitute Barney's. On the set, Dave Barras could be heard laughing as the drama ensued. He thought the whole idea was very funny. It was just realistic enough that I thought I caught Dave squirming a bit in his seat.

In the final segment, Barras's photo came off the wall and the beagle's went up. Karpowicz adjusted the frame and turned to the camera. "Nothing personal, Dave. The news is changing. We have to adapt to our viewers' needs."

How prophetic. I would experience that transition myself, but it would be fifteen years later.

Beagles and Burgers

I'd like to take credit along with Barney for our rise from the bottom of the AM ratings pile to the top, all the way to the number-one morning show in the mid-nineties. I can't, of course. Television shows live and die by the ratings, but research is expensive and there were no hard numbers that would pinpoint exactly what had happened. The rise did occur during my tenure. And, yeah, it also happened to coincide with Barney's rising popularity. Anyone who had a nose for the local news scene would have suspected that our growing success had at least something to do with the beagle. My success certainly did.

Barney gave me a different kind of TV presence from all the other reporters. A guy on another station doing a similar show pegged himself "Treeboy," often doing spots about gardening and home repair. That was his gig. I had mine. Fortunately, I was never pegged Dogboy. Not that I know of.

It wasn't long before booking the morning segment had to be done with an eye and a floppy ear toward Barney. He had touched a very deep chord with Hoosiers. Part of the attraction was the unpredictability of his behavior. But it was more than that. He was the devil in all of us, the unfulfilled desire to do bad things—not hateful, harmful things—but to be the imp, the rascal, the scamp. Barney was all of us when our mothers weren't watching.

The pressure to find something new to do during my time slot every morning, five days a week, was intense. And now I was also searching for a way to include the dog. I knew Barney's best moments would continue to depend on his unanticipated contributions. I also knew that giving him the proper environment to showcase his talent was a good show-biz move.

I didn't have to do much searching to find these ideas; they often found me. Many times the call came because the piece involved dogs, but the next step was always for me to find a way to involve Barney in the segment. Barney was seldom content with a cameo appearance, but he took what he could get. When I went back to the station to watch my segment on videotape, I'd see that even if Barney was not supposed to be part of the show, he managed to insinuate his nose or his tail into the camera shot. Viewers told me that watching my segment of the news was like the book *Where's Waldo?* Only it was *Where's Barney?* Keep your eyes open. He's there somewhere.

That summer I received one of the first calls requesting a personal appearance by the two of us. I'm not a very good businessman, and when I started getting these requests I didn't know how to respond to the question of compensation. What was I worth? How much did the dog raise the ante? Sometimes I'd put off the call by saying I needed to discuss this with my business partner. It sounded good, anyway. They just didn't realize I meant my dog.

The local Hardee's franchise owner had become a loyal fan of Barney's and he wanted the two of us to do a series of commercials and appearances to promote the restaurants.

His enthusiasm was so overwhelming that I bought into it. I could do what I did best—perform—and Barney would have center stage. Besides, Barney was a big fan of their sausage and biscuits, even devouring an entire plate for one of the future commercials.

The big test was whether stressed-out moms and dads would drag their kids out of bed on a Saturday morning to see Dick Wolfsie and his dog. It was true that we did have a lot of kids watching in the morning, more than the other stations, but news was still a grown-up deal, so I did have some question whether this would really work.

Convinced the kids would love the pooch, Hardee's did an extensive media blitz based on the Barney appearance. The biggest draw, they claimed, would be the giant billboard on the main drag in Muncie and in front of the store that proclaimed:

COME MEET DICK WOLFSIE AND BARNEY SATURDAY MORNING

That Saturday morning, Barney and I got up and headed north, about an hour's drive. The weather was great and I was hoping for a good turnout that would put me in good standing with Hardee's. But I was nervous. This could be a bust.

Barney and I arrived almost an hour early. Imagine my delight to see a full parking lot and a long line to get into the restaurant. There were hundreds of kids, balloons, clowns. It even looked like the parents were in a good mood.

"We're a hit," I said to Barney, who had already picked up the sausage scent and whose nose was twitching a mile a minute. My elation was short-lived, however. The owner was making his way toward me. I expected a big smile, but instead he looked as if he had just eaten a very bad fish sandwich. "What's the matter? The place is rocking," I said. "You should be thrilled."

"Yes, we have quite a crowd," he agreed. "But the parents thought you were coming with a dinosaur—a *purple* dinosaur."

Oops. We were in deep dino dung. Every parent in that parking lot had for the entire week been trumpeting to his preschooler that the child's dream was finally going to come true, that right there in little old Muncie, Indiana, the one and only internationally famous prehistoric reptile was going to make an appearance. Instead it was Dick Wolfsie . . . and his dog. Whoopee!

The tail went between the legs—mine, not the dog's. Barney was ready to party. I could now see fathers and mothers explaining to their disconsolate, dinosaur-starved children about how this very disappointing mix-up could occur. Oh, and the kids were very understanding, evidenced by the crying, screaming, and kicking that permeated the parking lot.

There had to be a way to make something positive out of this prehistoric debacle. I remember climbing back in the car and making a personal appeal to my buddy. "Let's go get 'em, partner. This is our first big test!"

Barney jumped out of the car and we headed for the fast-food eatery. It took just a couple of children to notice him. I held my breath. "Hey, it's a dog!" a youngster screamed. Then another: "Why is there a dog at Hardee's?" "That's the dog on TV," said my favorite kid of all. In violation of every health code, we walked into the restaurant. Barney hopped into one of the booths and sniffed the table, his wagging tail sticking through the space in the seat.

Now an even longer line had developed outside the restaurant. Probably not because Barney was there, but *any* line meant something cool was going on. Barney was in his heaven: sausage was in the air, belly rubs and ear strokes were as abundant as flaky biscuits, and suddenly, all was right in the fast-food world.

I knew we would never reach Barney the Purple Dinosaur status, but even an old fossil like me could see that entire families were responding to Barney in a unique way. Different, I think, than they would have to the TV cartoon figure. Many of the patrons had not even seen us on TV, but I sensed that each one felt as though Barney had come to see him or her. A one-to-one relationship with every single child.

And that's how it was for the next twelve years. No matter where Barney and I went, it never was staged or rehearsed. I never wanted it to be showbizzy. It was a not a public appearance. It was a personal visit, and everyone knew it.

Compare Barney to Nipper and Chipper, the two Jack Russells who represented corporate giant RCA. One of the earliest memories I have of a corporate logo was the old RCA image of the adorable Jack Russell terrier with the dark ears listening intently to a phonograph record over the caption, "His Master's Voice." The trademark painting was actually based on a real dog named Nipper who belonged to Francis Barraud, the artist who created it.

I was amused at several aspects of this marketing concept, which I witnessed firsthand when they made appearances in Indy. First, these dogs had no personality. Hyperactive? Yes. Character? Totally lacking. Charm? Zero. If Barney had been Mr. Barraud's model, the artist would have painted a beagle listening to his master's voice . . . and ignoring it.

And once the dogs playing Nipper and Chipper grew an inch or so, they had to be replaced by new dogs-in-waiting to retain their ever-youthful appearance to the public. If every time Barney gained a pound or two I had to replace him, it would have gotten very pricey and crowded at my house. Even odder was the fact that the trainer would not allow the public to pet the dogs, afraid that the *dogs* might get a disease.

What a concept: you schlep personality-deficient dogs around the country to publicize your product, but don't let people get too close to them or that might actually promote goodwill with your customers.

I'm glad I didn't get that memo. Barney's effect on people was all about his accessibility. Belly rubs and ear scratches were gratefully accepted and rewarded with rapid rotation of the tail and groans of pleasure. In public there were hardly any rules of engagement with Barney. No sticking the end of your lollipop in his ear. That was about it for guidelines.

And unlike Nipper and Chipper, Barney and I didn't sell a single TV. But we sure got people to watch it.

From Soupy to Nuts

Barney wasn't the first dog to appear regularly on television. But he may have been the first to appear as himself. Unlike Lassie and Rin Tin Tin and Yukon King, Barney went on without a script, without trainers or handlers, without a fictional character to hide behind. He didn't do his work in little pieces of scenes that were then assembled to make sense by an editor. For one thing, he never would have seen the point of doing the same thing over and over again until the humans decided it was right.

By helping to define me as an offbeat, out-of-the-ordinary reporter, Barney allowed me to do the kind of silliness I craved, even if Barney wasn't always the star . . . as in my second encounter with my childhood hero, Soupy Sales.

In 1996, Soupy called me from his home in New York City. He wanted to do some stand-up comedy in the Midwest. "Would anyone in Indianapolis be interested?" Honestly, I wasn't sure. The clubs were run by a younger generation, but fortunately Soupy's legacy had survived and the current owner of the main venue in town was a student of humor and knew who Soupy was. Or had been.

Soupy played Crackers Comedy Club in Indianapolis for a week in 1996. I saw almost every show, three of them a night. I ate lunch and dinner with Soupy for five days. "How am I doing?" he'd ask me over a big bowl of jambalaya at the old Dick Clark's restaurant.

"I'm the wrong person to ask," I told him. "I've seen the show eight times. Your jokes are old. I'm just laughing because you're Soupy Sales."

Soupy winked. "That's why I don't need new jokes."

While in town, Soupy made an appearance on WISH-TV's *Daybreak* where I did my three-minute segments on location each morning. And I did them live, just the way Soupy loved to do TV.

Soupy was fascinated with Barney. Not just the animal, but the concept. Soupy recognized that his entire career was based on the unpredictable, the uncontrollable, the improbable. The fact I would take a dog, especially an incorrigible one, on live TV during the news was a move right out of Soupy's playbook.

Of course, Soupy had two canines, albeit just puppets, who had each served as a comic nemesis. But the talking paws of White Fang and Black Tooth—actually barking and grunting—were subject to a modicum of scripting. Not Barney. I think that impressed Soupy, so much so that he requested that we use Barney during his appearance on Channel 8, just so Soupy could see how it all worked.

That morning from Soupy's hotel, I set up this premise: Soupy Sales was staying here and I had always wanted to meet him. Throughout the show, I asked guests in the lobby if anyone had seen Soupy Sales. No one had. Meanwhile, Barney sat on the lobby couch as if he were a hotel guest. In the final segment, I stood by as the elevator door slid open and out walked Soupy.

"Good morning," I said. "Have you heard Soupy Sales is staying here?"

Soupy did his imitable take to the camera. "I *am* Soupy Sales."

"No, seriously, the real Soupy Sales is supposed to be right here in the hotel," I said, feigning nonrecognition of the star.

"I'm Soupy Sales," he repeated, mocking frustration. Another take to the camera.

"Man, you sure got old," I said—a planned zinger, of course.

Suddenly (as precisely planned), a waiter walked by with a whipped cream pie in his raised hand. With pure comic grace, Soupy swept the pie from the waiter and deposited it squarely on my face. I had been hit with a pie by Soupy Sales.

Barney had no planned role in the comic sketch. Perched on the hotel lobby couch, he was content to simply watch the segment as it proceeded—until he discovered there was whipped cream slathered all over my face. No cue required from the cameraman. Barney leaped into my arms and starting licking the gooey stuff. I'm not even sure why I bothered bringing a towel.

Good Morning, Indianapolis!

Over the years, I'd battled the elements, technology, and human foibles (mostly my own) in an attempt to keep the show lively. I had made many reckless attempts to get laughs and ratings, but only once was I truly injured. Ignoring the warnings of a professional calliope player (a calliope is a type of pipe organ), I sat "inside" the organ and jumped to my feet, like a showgirl popping out of a cake, to start the show. In the process, the calliope pipes whacked me in the head. Blood gushed from my noggin and it appeared as though I was bleeding to death on live TV. The emergency room doctor couldn't suppress a smirk as he knitted my head together with eleven stitches. "Gee," he quipped, "this is my first calliope injury."

"Mine, too," I admitted.

Despite taking considerable risks for the good of the show, there are some things I wouldn't do—I'd just pretend I was doing them. I first learned the necessity of this ploy when I booked a segment on bungee jumping. The original plan was to bungee-jump from the top of a 700-foot platform. Great idea, except that I forgot to factor in four problems: I'm afraid of climbing, I'm afraid of heights, I'm afraid of falling, and I'm afraid of landing.

I'm also afraid of a dull show. Finally, we dressed a professional jumper in an outfit like mine and she (yes, *she*!) made the jump. At the end of the segment, anchor Dave Barras expressed skepticism, which was confirmed when my cameraman revealed that I was sitting in a lawn chair reading the newspaper during the jump. In case you think I'm a total wimp, it was the sports section.

A live TV spot coupled with on-air antics is a recipe for the unpredictable. There are no retakes on live television. Ask any reporter who has made it onto YouTube. When our remote truck failed during one show at a local dinner theater, I drove all the sisters from the play *Nunsense* back to WISH. The nuns invaded the studio and interrupted Vince, our sports anchor, by asking, "How is Holy Cross doing?"

Quick to the punch, Vince quipped, "Beat the devil out of William and Mary."

Another nun interrupted Randy, our weatherman, who had just forecast colder temperatures. "If this keeps up," spouted the sister, "you're going to have a bunch of blue nuns walking around."

In one Channel 8 segment, a fledgling band known as Dog Talk was slotted to play at a local pub. But the bar owner overslept and the musical instruments were locked inside the bar. Instead of canceling, I convinced the band to make do with assorted tin cans and other discarded items from the alley trash bin. It proved a winner, and the band went on to be one of the most successful musical groups in Central Indiana.

My favorite impromptu moment happened in front of a store on the west side of Indianapolis. When my scheduled guests didn't show, we pulled up in front of a local business called Discount Vacuum's. As a former English teacher, I had always been bothered by the unnecessary apostrophe in the sign.

And that became our show. I stopped people in cars and asked them what was wrong with the sign. "Are there two 'u's' in 'vacuum'?" several asked.

"Is one 'c' enough?" asked others. Finally, the store's owner saw his shop on TV and raced to the scene to ask what the problem was.

"It's your sign," I explained. "It's wrong."

The owner, visibly shaken, replied, "Oh, yeah? Show me a place in town you can buy them cheaper!"

Segments like these prove something I've said a thousand times: if you plan certain things, they will fail miserably. I was quick to deal with the unexpected. And I think that's why people watched me on the morning news. Then I added a dog to the mix. This was a train wreck waiting to happen. On the highway this is called rubbernecking. But people weren't viewing a crash, they were watching the news and, at least in those days, it worked.

Barney, of course, was my sidekick in so many of these moments. Like the one that involved the search and rescue arm of the Indiana State Police. The folks there were justly proud of their trained German shepherds, who could seek out a victim buried under rock, debris, or dirt in an explosion or building collapse.

The officers suggested on the phone that I be buried in the rocks at a nearby limestone quarry and that their dogs would be released to find me before I died of starvation or exposure. There wasn't much chance of this happening since the segments were only three minutes long. The idea of the dogs sniffing me out and then finding me sounded like good TV.

But what would Barney do on a mission like this? Could he compete with highly trained canines that did this for "a living"? Didn't matter. And that was the beauty of these segments. Either he'd be totally distracted and wander off to a local trash can (hey, that would be funny!) or he'd take his assignment seriously while the home viewer rooted for him. It was a no-brainer. An all-noser. It couldn't fail—unless it did. And how funny would that be? Are you with me?

That morning—cold and damp, as I remember—I opened the show with a serious look at the service these dogs performed and what a crucial role they played in public safety. This was always important to me. No matter how silly my interview ended up, I always felt a responsibility to pay attention to the guests' agenda and treat them with respect. That obligation met, let the fun begin.

During the second segment, just as the sun began to rise at about 6, my cameraman, Carl Finchum, perched himself on the giant limestone rocks while I burrowed into a crevice created by two adjacent limestone boulders. From the top of the pile, Carl pointed his camera back toward the parking area where Barney sat alongside several restless German shepherds who sensed they were about to go into action. One difference: we blindfolded Barney with a bandanna, hoping to handicap the competition and build the suspense. The idea of blindfolding a dog is just downright stupid. I knew that. In fact, that's why I did it.

All the shepherds stood by, drooling in anticipation as they awaited their command. Barney, agitated over my disappearance, was howling. Finally, all four dogs were released. They made a wide sweep of the area, spending several minutes snooping under every rock. Barney, whose departure we delayed to give him an additional disadvantage, hesitated for a moment, then made a direct line to me. Total time: forty seconds.

There are many possibilities for Barney's surprising success, none of which the dog trainers could explain. They were, I think, just a little miffed at Barney's natural ability. Amber, one of the officers, was good-natured about it as the show ended. "I think he peeked," she said.

A few weeks after Barney's search and rescue debut, I received a call from a local coonhound breeder interested in showing how his pride pack of four hounds could sniff and follow a fox scent to a tree. I remember smiling (an evil smile, at that) as the breeder explained the procedure. Once again, I was damn sure that this segment had Barney written all over it. It turned out to be the second most popular segment on the highlight tapes.

I met my guests at a southside Indianapolis park, where the dog coonhound owners dragged a raccoon scent along the ground, leading to a tree. "The dogs will follow the scent wherever it leads," bragged the owners. "They are very smart."

They are? It wasn't even a raccoon. It was just the scent . . . and you can't eat the scent. You just bark at it. I wasn't going to argue. Guys with coonhounds carry guns.

I bet Barney can go them one better, I thought. Barney could smell an unopened package of barbecue potato chips in my glove compartment.

Here was the plan: I brought this greasy summer sausage with me to the park and dragged it along the ground, right next to the raccoon scent. About fifty yards out, I had the two scents part. The raccoon smell led to the tree, and the beefy odor led to a picnic area where I placed the entire snack on top of a table.

Lights, camera, action! *Live* TV. The dogs were off. The four coonhounds rumbled ahead while Barney, who was beginning to sport a few extra pounds, managed to waddle up a sweat from behind. The coonhounds were dashing. Barney was lumbering.

The hounds realized that the raccoon scent was veering to the right. They followed in hot pursuit, panting in antici- pation of the kill. The kill? There was nothing in the tree. But they kept yapping at the empty limbs.

And Barney? Nose to the ground, he also veered, but to the left, and within seconds launched himself onto the picnic table, where he inhaled his greasy reward. He was Everyman . . . er . . . Everydog: the hero of the common canine, outdoing, outnosing, outsmarting the highly trained and expensive purebreds.

In my mind's ear, I could hear the viewers laughing and applauding for his good old midwestern common sense, cheering him on. "This is not just *your* dog, Dick Wolfsie," Hoosiers were saying. "Barney is our dog. And we are so proud of him."

The Escape Artist

Of course, first Barney was my dog. And despite what they may have wished, he was Brett and Mary Ellen's dog, as well. Sort of. I think as Mary Ellen observed my growing obsession with Barney, she realized I had become Frankenstein. I didn't set out to create a monster—it just came naturally. Okay, that's not true, either.

Yes, Barney was the monster because I had molded and shaped him. I accept the credit. My wife gives me the blame. With all the love that Barney enjoyed from the community, he created havoc at home. It wasn't so much the destruction he caused, but the distraction he became.

By the fall of 1994, Mary Ellen had gone back to Community Hospital full time as vice president of marketing. She had cut back at work after our son, Brett, was born, but now it was becoming more difficult for her to maintain her executive position as a part-timer. There was always more to do at the office, so what should have been four hours at work turned into an entire day. She was putting in forty hours and getting paid for twenty. She didn't need her MBA from the University of Michigan to know this was just silly.

Now back at the hospital every day, she realized that the

hours she spent with seven-year-old Brett had to be quality time—at least that was what she aspired to. It reminded me of a favorite *New Yorker* cartoon: A father has approached his son, who is playing a video game. The dad is clutching two baseball mitts and has, we assume, asked his son to play catch. His son replies: "Quality time? Do we have to, Dad?" Barney had made quality time almost impossible in our house. I saw trouble ahead.

Barney bonded with everybody he met, but he and Brett never connected. I don't think Brett was jealous. It was more a question of alternative lifestyles. Brett was a focused, play-by-the-rules young man who was ill at ease with unpredictability and chaos—Barney's two middle names. For example, Brett often squirreled away his favorite snacks in his bedroom so we wouldn't discover his craving for Chef Boyardee. He'd hide the easy-open cans under his bed. On more than one occasion, Barney also easily ate through the container, proving they were also easily gnawed through.

Barney seemed to have an obsession with Brett's room, sneaking in at night, knocking over the trash, and chewing his toys. One evening after a particularly tasty Italian dinner that Mary Ellen had prepared, we were puzzled by the disappearance of a huge loaf of Italian garlic bread we had left on the counter. We assumed the culprit was Barney because his breath was to die from. When Brett climbed into bed that night, be suddenly began to kick wildly at his sheets.

"Oh, yuck. This is, like, the grossest thing I have ever seen. I'm going to hurl!"

We were wrong, Barney had not devoured the entire crusty loaf; he'd decided to bury it, instead, under Brett's covers at the foot of his bed. The bread was wet, slimy, and half chewed. Crustiness was just a memory. On another occasion, Barney snooped into Brett's book bag and ate every No. 2 pencil he could dig out. My son, bless him, did find some humor in this. "Hey, Dad, when Barney does number two tonight, it's really going to be No. 2."

Brett finally installed a chain on his bedroom door because he thought, correctly so, that when Barney put his mind to it, he enjoyed full access to any place in the house. It was hard to criticize Brett's defensive behavior, considering that I had to duct tape the refrigerator door shut at night to prevent Barney from literally nosing his way into the meat bin.

Brett was unimpressed with the idea of Barney's celebrity. He was also unimpressed with mine. He once said to me, "Hey, Dad, you're on TV, radio, in the newspaper, and you write books. If you get your own Web site you can annoy people five different ways." I think he must have felt something akin to the way actress Candice Bergen recalls her own childhood as the daughter of famed ventriloquist Edgar Bergen, continually being asked how it felt to have a wooden dummy as a "brother." But Barney was flesh and blood and couldn't be hidden away in a closet, though Brett might have welcomed that option.

When people heard Brett's last name, they would ask if Barney was his dog. "No, he's my dad's dog," he would always say. A smirk would then follow, Brett's way of boasting that he, unlike the millions of other residents of Central Indiana, had not been hoodwinked by the mutt, as he called him. To Brett, Barney was a dog and nothing more. Except a pain in the ass.

It was ironic in a way. Here was a beagle that had become Central Indiana's dog, but my own son was distancing himself from him like a political candidate from his crazy uncle in the attic.

By contrast, Mary Ellen got a kick out of the fact that for the previous fifteen years, the mention of her last name had always resulted in the inevitable query, "Are you Dick's wife?" This was no longer the case. Now Mary Ellen was asked, "Are you Barney's mom?" Every time this happened in the grocery or department store, she took great delight in dashing home and dishing it out to me. For some reason, Mary Ellen liked being known as Barney's mother. Being known as Dick's wife? Not so much.

But the label "Barney's mom" was a bit awkward at times because fans of the show wanted my wife to sing the praises of Indiana's mascot, and that required a little lip-biting on her part. It was hard to break into song when the night before, the entire family had been scouring the neighborhood looking for Barney or cleaning up trash he had strewn all over the front yard after tipping over the garbage. Overall, Mary Ellen played the role effectively. Bad-mouthing the dog was not going to help my career.

Eventually, Mary Ellen would warm to the dog, though it was never the hot and heavy relationship it could have been. But she recognized Barney's value to me on TV.

Once when I caught her lavishing attention on Barney, actually on the floor hugging him, she put the whole thing in perspective. "I think he has finally made us more money than he has cost us." My wife, the business major.

I really am to blame for stunting Barney's potential as a family dog (meaning that the *entire* family loved him). My first big mistake was laughing when he was bad. Second, and this goes in hand with the first, I taught him that stealing food and destroying things was okay. In fact, I taught him tricks—tricks you don't want your family dog to do—by using food. I could manipulate the devil in the dog by simply providing the desired culinary treat at the proper time or in the appropriate place during a TV broadcast: a cookie on the edge of a table, a pepperoni stick in a boxing glove, or a biscuit in my pocket where the aroma of food would be evident. Or I'd give him something to tear apart on TV because people loved to see the terminator in action. Then, of course, he did the same thing at home.

Most dogs, for example, would not instinctively jump on the chair to procure the food from the table. That's more like chimpanzee behavior. But with a little help from his friendly coconspirator, Barney learned the technique. I encouraged his bad behavior. I rewarded it. Think of us as Barney and Clyde.

Why? It was funny. Damn funny. Whenever he stole a morsel, nosed into a cupboard, or had his way with a loaf of bread, the viewers loved it. "What a great dog." Everyone would say it. Everyone except Mary Ellen Wolfsie.

At first, my wife didn't understand why Barney could be bad on TV but not mend his evil ways back at our house. "When William Shatner gets home from shooting *Star Trek,* he knows he is no longer Captain Kirk, doesn't he?" This was not the best example she could have picked, but I understood her point.

In his beagle brain, every infraction of normal canine decorum not only went unpunished, but it was rewarded with laughter and permission to keep the bounty. I was a textbook enabler.

The result was that there was no way to discipline Barney at home. After all, the dog was only human. He didn't know he was just playing a bad dog on TV. When he was scolded for tipping over the trash in the garage, he appeared honestly puzzled. Hours earlier everyone had been laughing; now we were scolding him. "What gives?" he must have been saying. "Don't you people know how to raise a dog?"

And so Mary Ellen, who would have counted herself as a dog lover, initially counted herself out as a Barney fan. In the little time she had to devote to Brett—reading stories, helping with school projects, watching TV together—she was constantly being interrupted by the attention she had to pay to a dog who couldn't make up his mind whether he wanted to be more incorrigible in the house or in the yard, or wanted to make trouble four blocks away.

My wife would walk in the door at 5:30 PM and he'd be waiting for her arrival. To run away. He'd bolt out the door if she wasn't careful and scamper across the road to places unknown. Now what Mary Ellen had thought would be a quiet evening with Brett was instead another episode from the current series *Lost,* or *Without a Trace.*

Barney's escapes came in two forms: your common garden variety that resulted in a neighborhood adventure for him and us, and those that occurred during the TV show, a departure that I had to deal with live, on the air. Those were scary. And they happened often.

I sometimes wonder how my life, my career, would have been different if any of Barney's escapes had been successful. I never thought Barney was running away from me, but his wanderlust motivated him to look for every opportunity to enjoy a new adventure. I guess he just liked meeting new people, which is pretty much a beagle trait. But Barney clearly kicked it up a notch. On more than one occasion, he'd jump into a FedEx truck or the UPS van and enjoy the ride until the driver found him hiding in the back behind the parcels.

I do think that was part of the reason people embraced him. He was the free sprit in all of us, even if we couldn't express it or we lacked the opportunity to so indulge. Many of us would like to symbolically dig under that fence in our backyard to see if there's something out there we've been missing. Most of us never do it. Maybe some of you would like to run away with the UPS driver. That's none of my business.

Barney would bust loose from the leash during a walk, or sneak out through an unsecured door during a TV shoot. Twice at traffic lights he leapt through the open backseat window and bolted down the street. I'd chase him in the car, but then he'd veer off behind some houses and I would have to park the car and chase him on foot. Eventually, he'd be so taken by a scent that I could creep up behind him while his nose was buried in a hole or a bush. This was a game for Barney. He was good at it. I always hoped it was true that dogs aged seven times faster than humans, because it seemed like he was getting harder and harder to catch.

Barney never came back on his own. Usually someone would find him and call. Those conversations reminded me of the great O. Henry short story, "The Ransom of Red Chief," in which a couple of miscreants kidnapped an eight-year-old human bundle of aggravation, only to find that he was more trouble than any ransom was worth.

I always used a very scientific approach when looking for Barney. I would drive my car to each street corner, open up my window, and shout his name as loud as I could. To call this form of search useless would be giving the plan too much credit. In all his years, he never came when I called him. Never. I always found him. He always knew I would. *That* was the problem.

I'd scour the neighborhood with an eye toward open garbage pails or garages stocked with food supplies. Sometimes Barney would run off into the woods, but when he realized that most food in the woods is still alive and required some form of pursuit, his interest in the forest waned. But Barney knew every Weber grill in the neighborhood.

As I had done so many times, I'd retreat to the house without my sidekick—frustrated, empty-leashed, playing out in my mind what I would do if Barney was truly lost. Or worse, hit by a car. What would I tell the viewers? What would I tell my boss? I knew Brett would be able to deal with Barney's demise. Sure, he would have felt badly for me—he knew how much I loved Barney—but there was no question that a five-old-year old only child was going to find some satisfaction being top dog once again.

Sometimes when I would get home after an early evening meeting, Mary Ellen would meet me at the door. "He's at 34th and Fall Creek; someone just called. They were having a cookout and he showed up in their backyard. He's already had three bratwursts."

On the Road Again

Barney's most famous disappearance would become a true media event. It never quite rose to Jimmy Hoffa proportions, but in local lore it was pretty close.

One morning I was upstairs in my home office working on a TV segment when it dawned on me that I had not seen Barney for almost an hour. Not seeing him for that long was either a very good sign or a very bad sign. If he was asleep, the world was a safer place. If he was ambulatory, trouble was in the next room, or had been . . . or around the corner, or down the block, or who knew where.

I cased the entire house. No dog, and sure enough, the back screen door had a huge hole in it where Barney had ripped the wood partition to shreds. Yes, he had gotten out, had been out for up to an hour. This was not the kind of head start you want to give a beagle. I felt like the sheriff in *High Noon*. It was going to be tough to find a posse. No one in my house was going to sign up. I spent the rest of the day scouring the neighborhood alone.

I searched for him for an entire week. I placed signs within a three-mile radius of my neighborhood. The $100 reward generated a modicum of interest—not quite like the mug shots in the post office, but in both cases the culprits were slippery and on the run. Whenever I got a call suggesting he had been spotted, I'd head in that direction with a photo and a glimmer of hope. Nothing. Did people not know the difference between a beagle and a basset hound? Or did they think I didn't?

Many of the calls were about a beagle stray that lived downtown. I knew this was not Barney, but the little guy was quite a story himself. He had been living on the streets for several years, frequenting the back doors of local eateries. He was a survivor, a testimony to how a hound can make it on his own. Maybe Barney was rehearsing for his job.

My search did bring me into several, shall we say, transitional neighborhoods. "Have you seen this dog?" I'd ask, flashing his photo to a group of young hoodlums.

"Is he in trouble? What did he do? Are you a cop? Did he escape?"

"Yes, he escaped, but he's not a criminal. You guys are watching too much TV. I just want to find my dog."

Every radio station in town was now asking its listeners to keep an eye out for a stray beagle. The term "stray beagle" is considered redundant by anyone who knows anything about dogs. Over the six days, the on-air pleas and my ad in the local paper resulted in more than fifty calls from people who had either found or had seen a wayward beagle.

Several beagle rescue groups called to see if they could help by canvassing the pounds and humane societies. These volunteers are busy people—busier than, say, St. Bernard rescuers who, like Maytag repairmen, spend their time sitting around waiting for work. There just aren't a great number of lost St. Bernards in shelters, so the volunteers go out and rescue cocker spaniels and boxers every once in a while, just to keep their hand in the rescue business. Beagle rescuers are full-timers. Every beagle is a future escapee.

Some of the calls about Barney were downright bizarre. A vacationer in Florida called to tell me he saw a stray beagle at the Miami airport. Someone else claimed to have spotted Barney in a bookstore in North Carolina. I felt like the person in charge of logging Elvis sightings. People even called with female beagles, just in case I was confused. Or Barney was. One lady claimed she had seen Barney hanging around the NBC affiliate in town, implying, I guess, that he was thinking of breaking his contract and going with another station.

News director Lee Giles was concerned. It hadn't quite reached the point where the dog was *officially* a part of the morning show. Barney wasn't in the news open or used in station promotions. Oh, he was omnipresent on every show. An omnipresence that kept on giving.

After thirty years in the business, Giles's heart and head told him that the dog's absence from the program had caused quite a stir. But the decision was if and how to capitalize on his disappearance. If we milked his departure and he never returned, well, that was just a bummer for the audience. Not good for ratings and water-cooler talk. If he magically appeared one day, we'd seem like saviors. If we ignored the whole thing, maybe people would forget there was an adorable beagle puppy missing from the show. That would work. Yeah, right.

What did I want to do? I just wanted my dog back. Maybe Barney was on to a new life, a new doorstep. But in my gut, I knew that the dog and I had a deal—not a written contract, of course, but an emotional one. I knew it from day one. Call it a pre-pup agreement.

It was clear from viewer feedback that the audience was aware and anxious for updates. Radio disc jockeys asked their viewers to keep an eye out for the little bandit. *Daybreak* anchor Dave Barras inquired about Barney each morning during my first segment. I went to the Humane Society and the city pound every day in case he had been found. But after three days, I was losing hope.

I couldn't quite figure out how I felt during that time. If Barney was gone forever, I clearly had lost a business partner. But it was going to be tougher losing my best friend. I had never had a buddy at my side 24/7—man or beast. Or woman. I liked somebody sleeping next to me Sunday through Thursday, and that seat across from mine in the car was going to seem awfully empty. I stared at it for a week as I drove to work. It didn't seem possible he was gone. I wasn't sure I would find him. Maybe, just maybe, this time he'd find me. Like he did the first time.

Some of the calls and letters might have been pranks. It was hard to tell. But I had to take every sighting seriously. I could dismiss most of the tips after a brief conversation. A description of his coat markings, size, and weight were good clues whether this might have been Barney, but on several occasions, I needed to make a house call to confirm the identity of the dog. In many cases, the caller had simply seen a beagle in his or her vicinity, and while I did make a few excursions across town, I was convinced I'd never find him by willy-nilly combing a strange neighborhood.

He had to be relatively close to home—certainly within a few miles—so as a general rule, I did not respond to sightings outside our county. I deserved the dumber-than-a-box-of-biscuits award. He really could have been anywhere. Not only can beagles wander for miles, but I did not consider that he might have been picked up by someone in a car and transported across the county from Indy.

The magic call came on the seventh day of his disappearance. A lady in Southport, Indiana, was excited: "I think I have your dog, Mr. Wolfsie. I heard them talk about it on the radio."

"That can't be. Southport is twenty miles from my house."

She described the dog. It sounded like Barney, but no way. Not Southport. And he wasn't wearing a collar, which meant it couldn't be Barney. Thanks for calling. I was about to hang up, when something made me ask: "What else can you tell me about him?"

"Well, he howled all day, he jumped up and ate our dinner off the dining room table, he sleeps right next to me . . ."

"I'll be there in thirty minutes."

Sure enough, it was Barney. I was ecstatic. So was the lady who found him. She looked a little flustered. Was Barney happy to see me? No, he expected to see me. That was part of the game he played. I run away; you find me. He was probably miffed it took a whole week.

That was a Sunday afternoon and I decided to surprise the TV audience with his return on Monday morning during my segment on WISH-TV. I planned an entire segment where Barney would make a surprise entrance.

That evening, the phone rang. "Have you found your little friend?" an elderly woman inquired. "I've been so worried."

"Yes, I have," I said, beaming. "Aren't you nice to call? You can see us both tomorrow on TV."

"The dog will be on TV?"

"Yes, of course. Isn't that how you knew to call?"

"No, I'm eighty years old and don't watch TV. But I saw your ad in the paper. Every Sunday night I call everyone who's lost a pet just to see if they found their little friend. I'm glad you found him. I have six more calls to make. Bye."

The next morning, I did the morning show from my house. Barney made an entrance through my dining room doors. I could hear the cheers from the crew in the studio. I truly believed I could feel the sighs of relief all over central Indiana. I admit I milked his return for every "ooh" and "ahh" I could get. But everywhere I went for the next month, all people could say was, "I'm so glad he's back" "We were so worried" "What would you have done if you hadn't found him?"

A variation of that last question haunted me during Barney's entire life. What was I without Barney?

Did Barney really walk to Southport? Even I doubt that. He hitched a ride from someone, jumped onto a UPS truck, or hopped into the backseat of a 4x4, then hopped back out at the first stop. The lady who found him said he'd just appeared on her front step and howled to come in. That was Barney. He did not relish spending the evening outside in the cold. He knew he had to find a hot meal and a warm body to sleep next to. It was simply a matter of charming the pants off someone. And he was very good at that. He could do that to anyone.

Except Mary Ellen. She always saw through *both* of us. A common question fielded by my wife over the years was: "Is he the same at home as on TV?" This, of course, was usually in reference to Barney, not me. But when Mary Ellen wasn't sure who the questioner meant, she simply said "high maintenance," which pretty much covered all bases.

Sometimes she used the terms *loyal, loving,* and *good with people.* I guess I had never realized how similar the dog and I were. There was one difference. Except when I accidentally threw away my paycheck, Mary Ellen seldom caught me in the garbage.

When we moved into a new house in the mid-nineties we solved one of our major problems: Barney's running away. We installed an electric fence, which delivers a mild zap if your pet tries to venture outside the parameters of the yard. With Barney's wanderlust now controlled, he seemed to mellow a bit, especially as he aged. But he only mellowed at home. Not at work.

At each new remote location, his natural beagle curiosity led him into constant exploration because there were always new people to meet, or maybe people *with* meat. But back at the house, once he had established that there was no way to score a treat and had been gently reminded by his electric collar that he was confined to the yard, he took the option I always favored when my basic desires were thwarted: He took a nap.

Unlike his daily excursions with me, home had become a bit old hat. Except for an occasional surprise visitor at the front door, life was mundane. His breeding required the equivalent of a fox hunt each morning to get the juices flowing. That mission was accomplished on TV. Then it was back to the lair—*zzzzzzzzzzzzzz*. He seldom watched TV, although I was struck over the years at how many people sent me photos of their dogs watching Barney on the boob tube.

Barney followed me around from room to room, always preferring to nap within a few feet of my location. This allowed him to lobby for inclusion in any errands I had to run around town. He'd sit up on his back legs and howl at me when I put on my shoes. I was a soft touch. I never went anywhere without him.

On occasion, he'd nest next to Mary Ellen on the couch, especially if I had to leave the house without him. Barney seldom had much to do with Brett, who continued to believe that cats were where it was at.

Brett was never cruel to Barney. Not once. It was simply a loveless, arranged marriage. Brett had an unspoken deal with this devil: I'll stay out of your face; you stay out of my room.

That was the reality of life at home. Some people may have thought that Barney was a laugh a minute 24/7. That he led some kind of celebrity life. It wasn't that he was a different dog at home; it was simply that he *was* a dog at home. Not always a well-behaved one, but still a dog.

Taking a Dive

Early in 1994, I did a segment from the swimming championships at the Natatorium in downtown Indy. This seemed like a place where it would be safe to let him roam. The area was enclosed, no trash was visible anywhere, and Barney did not like to swim—so I knew he wouldn't skirt the edge of the water and sniff around. I figured he'd be a touch disappointed when, unlike other places with pools we had visited, there were no beach chairs for him to sack out in once snuffle patrol was over.

As was often the case, once I got into a TV interview that did not specifically require the dog, I would temporarily forget his whereabouts, focusing instead on the task at hand. This time my conversations were with the swimming officials and a few of the athletes.

I was often faced with a kind of catch-22. Recognizing Barney's thirst for exploration, I knew it was necessary to let him wander during the TV segments. Tying him up restricted his troublemaking nature, but that, I realized quickly, was what viewers wanted to see. Even inside a building he could get into a lot of trouble. He'd investigate every nook and cranny, climbing back staircases and snooping in areas that were clearly off limits. Call it rubbernecking or beagle-necking, people tuned in every morning to see the havoc that was going to be wrought.

During the brief interview with the Purdue University diving coach, I noticed Carl, my photographer, trying to suppress a laugh, although there seemed to also be a touch of horror in his expression. If you are shooting live television and your photographer is laughing while you are on camera and there is nothing amusing going on that you are aware of, it is safe to say that there is something amusing going on you are not aware of. Like your fly is open.

Because of the informality of my segment and the morning show in general, I often talked directly to the cameraman while the show was in progress, something that is not a conventional practice on most news shows.

Carl, by the way, did with Barney and me what any good photographer does with a reporter . . . or any fashion photographer does with a model. Carl came to understand the personality of his two subjects.

Carl seldom knew what I was going to do next—nor did I—and no one ever knew what Barney was up to. Carl had to be ready for the unexpected. As the years progressed, he and I started to think the same way. Like married couples. He'd anticipate my next move; after the show he'd say, "I knew where you were going with that."

Sometimes I'd throw Carl a curve by darting to a different location across the room, or requesting live on the air that he pan his camera quickly to the right or left. In the context of the show, this spontaneity worked just fine.

Barney and Carl bonded. If Barney was bored with his surroundings, he would sit right at Carl's feet. But when Barney roamed during the segment, Carl kept one eye on the dog, in case he did anything newsworthy or, more important, something funny. At that point, the camera would zero in on the real star.

But back to the Natatorium. "What's the matter, Carl?" I asked on camera, assuming that his facial expression had something to do with Barney. With that, Carl tilted the camera toward the diving board just above my left shoulder. There, at the very end of the sixty-foot diving platform, looking out over the pool, was Barney.

"Oh, my God!" I screamed. "How the hell did he get up there?"

You try to restrict references to hell on TV unless you are a televangelist, but this seemed quite an appropriate use of the expletive. I dropped the microphone in the middle of the interview and bolted for the platform. In my mind, I could hear people all over the city gasping—okay, maybe a few laughing—but this scene had serious consequences written all over it. A first-time platform dive for either the dog or me in front of tens of thousands of people was not good PR for the station. Even if he scored a 10.

You're probably wondering how a dog climbs a sixty-foot ladder. I wondered the same thing as I broke into a sweat galloping toward the diving apparatus.

No, Barney didn't climb a ladder. Entrance to the diving boards and platforms are via traditional stairs, a safety precaution for the athletes—and apparently beagles, as well.

Nevertheless, Barney was now literally living on the edge. He was looking over the platform. What was he thinking? I didn't want to know.

I scrambled up the staircase to the entrance of the diving platform. Barney turned his head back over his shoulder with a perplexed look on his face, if that's possible with a dog. He certainly had no intention of jumping. Or did he? And were we still on live TV? Would he come to me when I called him? Well, that hadn't happened since ... well, ever. I rummaged through my pants. I often carried bits of human food in my pocket to lure him back to me in situations like this—not that there had ever been a situation like this.

Sure enough, tiny slices of pepperoni in the fold of my front pocket. As I waved them at him, the spicy odor wafted to his nose. Barney carefully—very carefully—turned and walked back toward me.

If your doctor ever tells you that pepperoni is not good for your health, you may repeat this story. It prevented my heart attack.

I always had mixed feelings about whether to share on TV the fact that Barney had gone missing, especially if it occurred while we were on the air. What would the viewers think? Barney didn't love me? I wasn't careful enough watching him? In some cases, his disappearance and his mischief led to some great television. When left to meander inside a building, Barney could, despite his girth, manage to squeeze his way through any aperture. If he couldn't find an open door, Barney would find an unsuspecting accomplice, roll his big brown eyes, and convince someone that he required some assistance in vacating the premises.

Yes, Barney had a great many famous escapes, but he also had some dramatic rescues. At least once a week, Barney fans still come up to me and boast that they once found Barney at a Burger King, or they rescued Barney from a prickly bush, or they found Barney in their garage. That was part of the allure. So many felt a connection to him. He wasn't just a name on a page or even a dog on TV. There were scores of people who could honestly say: "If it weren't for me, Barney might have been lost forever."

He was almost lost forever in Greenwood, Indiana, during a show. My major mistake that morning? I asked a sixteen-year-old boy who was there with his fifteen-year-old girlfriend to watch Barney while I did my segment. That's right: I requested that teenagers take some responsibility, to keep their paws off each other for two hours and instead watch four canine paws. I guess I didn't learn anything teaching high school for nine years.

After the first segment, I asked my helpers where Barney had gone. "We haven't seen him," they said in exact unison, a good indication they were more into each other than scrupulous surveillance of the dog.

"*You haven't seen him?*" I bellowed. "Excuse me, but what exactly do you mean by 'you haven't seen him'? You were supposed to watch him, isn't that right?"

"Well, we didn't think he'd run away. The door was half-closed."

"It was also half-open," I pointed out, but this was a subtle distinction to be sure, and one that apparently had escaped this dynamic duo.

I panicked. This was always my first mode of response. Based on past experience, Barney could travel half a mile in about six minutes . . . unless he stopped to tip over a trash can or pick up some fast food on the way.

I ran up and down Meridian Street, the main thoroughfare in town, hollering his name. Cars whizzed by and a thunderstorm had rolled in. As always, my mind flashed forward to how I would deal with his disappearance on the air. Or what I would say if the unthinkable happened on that busy street where huge vehicles barreled by every second.

I called the local police chief and begged him to put out an APB. I wasn't sure what an APB was, but I knew the police took it seriously. Maybe they would find Barney.

Incredibly, the chief agreed to do it—further proof, I guess, that the dog enjoyed a certain status in the community. If my wife had called and said I was missing, there would have been a two-day waiting period before valuable police resources were squandered on a guy who had just made a wrong turn. Or had been kidnapped. I kept checking back with the police, but there had been some kind of bank robbery across town and, understandably, a lost dog had ceased to be a priority.

An hour later, still no Barney. And no previous experience to suggest he would return on his own. I was about to head home. Suddenly, police sirens and swirling colored lights. The police car rounded the corner at about 70 mph and skidded to a halt next to me in the mall parking lot. *Oh, no,* I thought, *he wasn't hit by a car. Please, God, no.*

I looked in the vehicle. Sitting next to the officer was Barney. Both his front and back paws were locked securely in handcuffs. Barney looked guilty, like most people do in the back of a police car. And he was guilty. Of being Barney.

"What happened, Officer?"

"Your dog has been arrested."

"For what?"

"I was off duty and went to the supermarket to get some milk for my family. I look up and there's your dog walking down aisle 4 with a barbecued chicken in his mouth. He's in serious trouble, Mr. Wolfsie. Hoosiers don't take chicken stealing lightly."

Barney was remanded to me. The people at the supermarket were very nice and no theft charges were pressed.

Barney would have hated prison food. But he would have eaten it. The fact is, Barney would eat anything. Even though I was in the communication business, I wasn't very successful in making people understand that nothing was safe from his jaws if it was in the same ZIP code. But nobody ever believed me. Part of the problem was that many of the guests had never lived with a beagle before, so my concerns seemed a bit overwrought. Part of it was just people's almost instantaneous affection toward him. He was so cute, so lovable. How could he ever do anything wrong? Were these people not watching television? Had they not seen him in action?

The Food of the Gods . . . er . . . Dogs

Those who don't have dogs may not fully appreciate how motivated animals can be when it comes to food. Their obsession is understandable. Dogs sleep, wait for you . . . and eat.

No matter where I took Barney, I tried to take extra care in limiting his exposure to anything edible. I was just as nervous when it came to things that were not edible, but you can't hide a couch or a table leg. He was very willing to taste anything.

When I arrived at my location each morning, I walked in with Barney, his tail wagging in anticipation of a new adventure. Barney reminded me of an FBI agent who was not apt to exchange any pleasantries or conversation until every portion of the environment had been checked first for anything amiss, like a bomb or listening device.

Before Barney would officially greet the guest, he would scrutinize with his supersensitive nose every corner of every room; he would knock over every trash basket and nose up to every table his nose could reach, often balancing on his hind legs to get a better view of the landscape. Once that was accomplished, he'd reappear and interact with humans. That was his MO. It never varied.

I knew when I entered someone's house or place of business that I had to prevent any potential trouble that could harm Barney. "Are there any animal traps in the place? Is there any rat poison he could get to?" That's how I started. I took no chances.

Then it was time to protect the guest. "Is there any human food in the garbage or elsewhere that this dog could reach considering he can open a refrigerator door with his nose, and climb up on a chair to get on a table. DO YOU UNDERSTAND WHAT I AM SAYING? NOTHING IS SAFE. *Nothing.*" I usually calmed down at the end of the rants so people didn't think I was a lunatic.

This approach never worked. People don't have a very good perception of what accessible rations are stashed about their surroundings. On one St. Patrick's Day, Barney and I paid a visit to a local retail shop that specialized in everything Irish. The woman and her daughter were big Barney fans and even brought their Irish wolfhound to meet Barney. We walked in, and I said (and this may sound a little familiar) . . .

"Is there any human food, in the garbage or otherwise, that this dog could reach considering he can open a refrigerator door with his nose, and climb up on a chair to get to a table. DO YOU UNDERSTAND WHAT I AM SAYING? NOTHING IS SAFE. *Nothing.*"

"I don't think so," said the Irish lady. Then she glanced at her twelve-year-old daughter, who gave a shrug, which was probably a clue I should have done my own investigation.

The show went well, although I was distracted because I was trying to keep a careful eye on the expensive Irish cashmere scarves that were displayed at beagle level. The scarves did not appear to be digestible, but that distinction could never be confirmed until Barney had eaten something.

I did think it odd that Barney was not lurking during the segment. I figured it was because the Irish wolfhound, although a gentle giant the size of a pony, had pretty much scared the heck out of him, and Barney had gone somewhere to hide.

As the segment ended, the Irish lady's daughter motioned to her mother.

"Mom," she whispered, "where are those four sticks of butter for the cookies we're going to bake?"

I turned red. Green would have been more appropriate for St. Patrick's Day.

"You told me there was no food out!" I barked.

"Well," said the store owner, a touch indignant, "I didn't think he'd eat four sticks of butter."

"Oh, I see. You thought he was on a low-fat diet?"

I always tried to avoid even the hint of exasperation with guests, but incidents like this really tested my patience. Jeez, a pound of butter. It couldn't have been a worse food choice. At least Barney wasn't lactose intolerant.

I herded Barney into the car. We had a speaking engagement at 10 that morning in Columbus, Indiana, about ninety minutes away. I'm obviously no expert on animal digestion, but I do have a suggestion: don't travel in a car for almost two hours with a dog that has just eaten four sticks of butter. Enough said.

A month later we paid a visit to an office complex where I was to interview the CEO of a new company. The secretary greeted us at the door and gave Barney a hug, the only thing that ever deterred him temporarily from his customary routine of wall-to-wall inspection.

That's when I told her . . . well, I think you know what I told her.

"Oh, heavens no," she said. "We never keep food around. That's unsanitary."

Ten minutes later, the boss, who had returned to his office for a brochure, informed his secretary, "Rita, I think Barney ate the cheese Danishes that were on my desk."

Rita's response was a classic. "Both of them?"

Yes, Rita. Both of them. Go figure. And he was supposed to be watching his figure. I turned so she wouldn't see me grinning. Rat poison is not funny. Four sticks of butter, not funny. Two cheese Danishes? Very funny.

The dog's obsession with food was hilarious on TV, humorous at the State Fair, and a hoot at the television station, but it didn't go down well with Mary Ellen and Brett, who also never quite understood how nimble a hound can be when aromatically motivated. I sometimes thought that Barney's periodic escapes from the house were the only respite we had from his gluttonous ways. For a while, he was someone else's problem.

And so much of it was our fault. Leave the garage door open and every trash can was upturned; forget to close the pantry door and anything on the floor was fair game. (Actual game, by the way, was of no interest to him. He was scared of moving food.) We finally realized the only way to keep him from prying the refrigerator door open with his nose and using his head as a lever to complete the operation was to duct tape the door shut.

It would be hard to estimate how many potential dinners (raw food on the counter) and actual dinners (meals on the dining room table) Barney managed to negotiate into his belly. Nothing ticked off Mary Ellen and Brett more than this (to me, understandable) affinity for human food. I called it natural behavior. And ironically, it should have been easy to prevent. Push the food back farther on the counter. How hard could that be? And yet, we could never get it through our thick Homo sapiens skulls. Countless times even our take-out dinners never made it home. Once after putting a bucket of KFC in the backseat, I ran into the liquor store for some beer. Barney didn't require a personal dinner invitation from the Colonel. That night we had mostly beer for dinner. Barney never read the owner's manual about not eating chicken bones. And I never got the memo that dog owners need behavior modification more than dogs. They really should call it human obedience school.

And again, no amount of discipline was going to make a difference. Why? Because the next day on-air I would reward him for this very same atrocious behavior. Barney knew if he could deliver a laugh, he was earning his kibble.

And speaking of delivery, I discovered that Barney loved pizza the week Mary Ellen was on a long business trip. She said it was to earn a living but it was more likely to seek a beagle-free zone. I was left to care for my son even though I don't think Mary Ellen fully trusted me alone with Brett, then ten years old, and the dog.

To make me feel more comfortable, Mary Ellen gave me a detailed list of do's and don'ts. If I was unsure about anything, she told me, I was to consult the list. Everything—yes, everything—was in alphabetical order. Some examples:

B: Bedtime (You both need to do this every night. Do not skip a night.)

D: Dishes (Wash after each meal in dishwasher. Do not mix dishes and underwear in same load.)

M: Meals (To be eaten while seated—not in the car, and not standing at the sink. Space them out over the day.)

V: Vacuum Cleaner (About three feet tall, with a long bag attached to it and a hose coming out the side. I don't expect you to use it, but I didn't want it to scare you if you opened the closet by mistake.)

X: Xylophone (It's the only word I know with the letter X. You may play one while I am gone.)

She also made it quite clear that she expected Brett and me to eat healthy meals. So that Friday night, I ordered an extra-large pizza from Noble Roman's with toppings representing all the major food groups. The pizza was big enough for the next three dinners and a couple of breakfasts. The phone rang as Brett and I sat at the kitchen table.

"It's probably Mom," I said. "I'm going upstairs to take the call. Watch the pizza."

It would be about ten minutes before I first realized what part of "I'm going upstairs to take the call. Watch the pizza," Brett paid no attention to. At first I thought he'd headed back to his homework, but I had confused him with the boy next door. No, he apparently still had four hours left on his Nintendo game.

When I returned to the kitchen, there was no pizza left. And no box. And I knew that Brett seldom ate the box, so it must have been the canine trash compactor.

The culprit was hiding behind the couch, which was apparently tough for him because before he ate the pizza he weighed forty pounds and now he was tipping the scales at forty-five pounds. He was stuck, wedged between the sofa and table. He was gasping. Hopefully, I thought, it was an errant piece of mozzarella that would work its way down and nothing to worry about, but on more careful analysis I decided it was best to panic.

I got Barney from behind the couch and tried to get him to walk, but Barney's tummy was so distended that it scraped along the ground like a basset hound's ears. His stomach was making strange gurgling sounds as though it was about to erupt like a volcano.

Now I figured I had to get all that pizza out of him. I wasn't sure why this was a good idea, but it gave me a sense I was doing something. I had read about it in some pet first-aid book, but I had confused in my mind the appropriate over-the-counter drug that would accomplish this. I had a sneaking feeling that the difference between hydrogen peroxide, sodium bicarbonate, and hydrogen chloride was pretty significant. It was one of the three, but I couldn't be sure. But I did remember it was two teaspoons. Of what, I didn't know.

I ran to the phone and called Barney's vet, Dr. McCune, who answered the phone from a dead sleep at his home. Charlie Bob, as his friends called him, was a great guy with forty years' experience. But could he handle an emergency of this breadth and magnitude?

"Doc, it's Dick Wolfsie."

"What's the matter, Dick? It's awfully late."

"Barney just ate an extra-large pepperoni pizza. What should I give him?"

There was pause. I'm sure that he too, at this hour, was trying to remember the difference between hydrogen peroxide, sodium bicarbonate, and hydrogen chloride.

"Doc," I repeated, "what should I give him?"

"A Budweiser?"

Then he hung up the phone. All great comedy lines require the proper denouement. The click of the phone beautifully framed the irony of the situation, highlighting my hopelessness, my frustration, and my sense of futility.

Clearly this was not the emergency I thought it was. As Dr. McCune would later explain, the treatment for Barney was the same as for humans: do nothing and let the patient vomit. For two hours.

I have to admit. It worked like a charm.

Usually after an experience like this I would promise myself that the next time Barney ingested something I considered inappropriate, I would just kick back and chill. The dog had ingested so many things, his stomach had clearly made the necessary accommodations. But two weeks later, another crisis.

It was Friday night—actually very early on Saturday morning. "What's that noise downstairs?" asked Mary Ellen. I loved questions like that. Either it was a burglar or it was nothing. And either way, I had no intention of going downstairs. I sat up in bed and it was clear that it was Barney snooping around in the kitchen, grazing for food. Barney had sometimes made his way down the steps in the middle of the night to see if he could rustle up a snack, so I figured he was pawing at the pantry door where his treats were kept.

I stumbled down to the kitchen and there was Barney chewing on what appeared to be a piece of aluminum foil. No, it was an ant trap that the beagle had negotiated from beneath the fridge with his paw! The blue "poison" was dripping from his mouth.

Again, my career flashed before me along with the headlines of the next day: BARNEY POISONED. ANTS MOVE BACK UNDER FRIDGE.

I wrestled him into the car and raced to a local twenty-four-hour pet emergency clinic just a few minutes away. It was 3 in the morning and I began ringing the bell, then banging on the door. The on-call veterinarian, who had been sleeping prior to my interruption, hastened to the entrance. She peeked through the peephole in the door. Unfortunately, she recognized me.

"What is it, Mr. Wolfsie? Is Barney okay?"

"He ate an ant trap. Is he going to die?" I watched her expression. She didn't seem to be taking my extreme angst very seriously.

"Heavens no," said the vet. "Those things don't even kill ants."

I once composed a list of the ten most interesting things he ever ate. None of these things ever caused any distress. Except in me. This is not to say that there wasn't evidence wafting in the air that he had been naughty, but there was just as much proof he had remained healthy despite some very unorthodox ingestions.

The Top Ten Things He Ate★

1. Four sticks of butter at one time
2. An entire bucket of KFC I left on my backseat (remember)
3. Half a turkey on Thanksgiving Day
4. An entire platter of lasagna (Garfield, eat your heart out)
5. Two packages of hot dog buns

★ As determined by an independent Lab, his best friend.

6. A head of lettuce
7. Two cherry pies
8. A box of chocolate cherries (I know he's not supposed to eat chocolate. But he didn't know that)
9. That $25 giant pepperoni pizza, including the box
10. An entire loaf of Italian bread (Well, not the whole loaf. He buried the rest under the blankets at the foot of Brett's bed.)

A final note of pride: Emergency veterinarians tell me it is not uncommon for beagles to enjoy batteries, dental floss, and sweat socks, each of which requires invasive surgery to save the animal. Barney generally restricted his diet to human food, the ant trap being a notable exception.

Oh, and by the way, it's hydrogen peroxide. One teaspoon of 3 percent hydrogen peroxide (make sure the strength is not any higher than 3 percent) per each ten pounds of body weight. Just in case you find a beagle. Or a beagle finds you.

Is that a Wet Nose in My Popcorn?

Barney was more than a TV hound. He was a multimedia megastar who found his way into just about every medium there was.

He appeared on the cover of the city magazine *Indianapolis Monthly* three times. Give me a second here while I figure out how many times I was on the cover. . . . Okay, never.

In one edition, the publishers wanted to highlight the major symbols of the Circle City, Indianapolis. They put only three icons on the cover: A basketball, a race car, and a photo of Barney. Talk about being in good company!

Barney was also a Hollywood movie star. Not Hollywood, California, but the Hollywood Bar and Filmworks in downtown Indy. It has since moved to Chicago, but in its day it was the yuppie place to go in town, the one theater where you could see a movie and sip Merlot at the same time.

The owner, Ted Baltuch, like any smart hotel owner, knew that seats with no people in them, like rooms with no guests, did little for the bottom line, so to speak. As a result, he gave away free tickets to Saturday and Sunday kids' matinee movies. The hope was that burger-and-fries sales would cover his expenses and introduce the theater to the children's parents—who might then return without kids.

For several years, I would mention the freebie on the morning show, as well as the additional incentive of meeting Barney and me before the movie. Kids could pet Barney and get autographed photos of the two of us. With the help of a good flick (*Toy Story*, for example), it was not uncommon to sign two hundred pictures during the hour preceding the show. Ted paid me for my appearance, and Barney was belly-rubbed for sixty minutes. I think he got the better deal.

Ted knew that the parents—the ones who watched the news—were usually more interested in the trip to meet Barney for the celebrity angle than the kids, many of whom just loved dogs in general. But I did notice as time went on that more and more children were watching our news, in part motivated by their chance to see Barney.

Success in television requires a constant influx of viewers, a curious blend of keeping the old and attracting the young, although for the past few years, keeping the older viewer has lessened in priority. Of course, TV stations now sell a lot of Viagra ad slots, suggesting not all TV fans are twenty-some-things.

The news executives at WISH-TV later felt that a dog on the news skewed toward older viewers. But ironically, many of those youngsters who had encounters with Barney are now young adults with their own families. "I grew up watching you and Barney!" a young woman will tell me with her two toddlers at her side. Sometimes I can't believe I have spanned an entire generation on TV. At this point I have kept my face on TV in Indy for about a century. At least in dog years.

Ted had another idea: how about if Barney and I appeared in a short piece of film that would welcome guests to the theater? The clip would explain some of the required information for the movie guests: Smoking rules, NO TALKING, fire exits, NO TALKING, bathroom locations, NO TALKING.

Shooting the spot required that I recite those basic theater rules on camera. Throughout my television and radio career I have been blessed with the gift of ad-lib, but God did curse me with zero capacity to remember prewritten lines. While I struggled with the script, I sat there with a bag of buttered popcorn as a prop, which drove Barney insane. Just when I was about to do Take No. 42, Barney would bury his nose in the popcorn, scattering the kernels all over the table. I'd forget my lines and the director would yell, "Cut! Take 43."

Well, how dense was I? Barney had found the perfect vehicle to inject humor into this otherwise rather vanilla presentation. Okay, now this *was* my idea. To ensure his total obsession with the popcorn, I added a chicken wing to the bottom of the box and situated the treat right under his nose.

Take 44: I still stumbled with my wording, but that was okay because I had clearly been distracted by the popcorn pooch. "Leave my popcorn alone," I continually admonished him, but to no avail. In the video, his entire head is buried in the popcorn box. All you see are ears flopping over the box.

The more Barney tried to exhume that hidden chicken wing, the funnier it got. Take 45 completed the shoot. I liked working with a pro. That movie introduction ran thousands of times over the years. Whenever I would visit the theater, I'd enjoy it as people laughed at the movie opening.

Barney's success on the big screen led to more success for him on the little screen, which was based on what Channel 8 was showing on the big screen. I'd better explain.

General Manager Paul Karpowicz's feelings about Barney grew more positive over the years, so much so that he began to think about additional ways to capitalize on the dog's popularity.

WISH-TV had a stockpile of old movies, films that had been purchased but were just taking up space in the studio basement. Others were part of an old rental agreement that we were contractually stuck with. Some were good, but many clearly were in the B-movie category. What did the B stand for? "Maybe it stands for beagle," surmised Karpowicz, who suggested to me one day that we do a late-night show called—are you ready for this?—*Barney's Bad Movies*.

A gutsy move, really. We were advertising that the movies were stinko, but by putting Barney's name on the program, it might attract a bit more attention in that late-night slot where ratings had waned on the weekends.

But wait. It was more than just the title for a show. We built this elaborate set with movie lights, an old movie projector, and a doghouse. And a fire hydrant that I borrowed from the city. There was a desk for me and a chair for the hound. This was real showbiz. No expense was spared. That's because we had no money. We built the set from stuff people brought in. Kim Gratz, one of the producers, was assigned the project. She had no idea how this was going to work. And that was twice as much as I knew.

We decided that Barney should have an actual role in rating the weekly movies. For each film, we would prerecord what is called a wrap-around (TV talk for an intro and "outro" to the movie). Usually we'd make fun of the movie, but we'd always feature Barney in some quirky, offbeat way. If the movie was really bad, we'd take shots of Barney sleeping, usually on his back, and put them in the corner of the screen during the picture. Then when it was over we'd rate the movie with—yeah, you guessed it—one to four fire hydrants. Okay, so you didn't guess it.

Barney jumped on the couch and really did sleep through every movie, not unlike our viewers, I'm quite sure. The ratings did not rise appreciably, but Karpowicz's contention was—quite clever, really—that even if people didn't watch the flick, they'd see the promos and word would spread about this off-the-wall idea. People would talk about WISH-TV. And maybe that would boost ratings in the morning.

Over the five-year run we even had special guests like Indianapolis Mayor Steve Goldsmith, Michael Medved (the film critic), Boomer (the Pacers mascot), Soupy Sales, and many of the Channel 8 reporters. Patty Spitler, the station film critic, made several appearances, often to defend the movie and spar with Barney over his fire hydrant ratings. Patty was much more forgiving. Barney was a tough critic, but even-pawed. He slept through everything.

Well, not everything. During one commercial break he realized it was a real fire hydrant on the set and he reacted appropriately, especially considering the quality of the movie.

One Friday night we showed *Patton*, starring George C. Scott. This was a far better movie than our usual fare, so to celebrate, I dressed as a WWII general and we even found a K-9 Army uniform for Barney. Sadly, he only got to be a corporal, one of the few times I outranked him. At the breaks, I barked orders to Barney to *sit, stay, come.* I don't think he would have listened to the real Patton, either.

Barney's Bad Movies ran almost four years, but after Karpowicz left, the new boss didn't have quite the same commitment to the idea, it not being his and all. Barney finally lost his gig, the victim of poor ratings and the end of our film rights to many of the flops.

That's showbiz, even if you're a dog.

TV, movies, magazines. What about radio? Even the growing popularity of Barney could not buffer me from what was almost a career and personal disaster in 1994, a year that threatened my relationship with my son, my wife, and the potential for a growing fan base. There were times when I thought that Barney was my only friend.

The Rush of Radio

I was content with my job at WISH but recognized that I was still basically a talk show host at heart. Morning pieces were two minutes long but embarrassingly short in content. Sure, I did some innovative things, stuff that most others would not have dared do on live TV, but the segments were basically sound bites—nothing more than a snapshot of an issue or upcoming event. It was a break from what was often a typical morning newscast, chock-full of natural disasters, murders, and stock traffic reports. The morning team at WISH was clearly the loosest and most informal of all the anchors on the different stations, but news was basically serious.

I often thought back to my previous stints when I'd been interviewing politicians, doctors, and lawyers; people with dramatic personal stories who might have spent an hour on the couch next to me. The show was often about just one issue. It was educational. I enjoyed that role. It lit up the teacher in me.

My role at WISH was a blast. I did love getting laughs and creating on-the-spot lunacy each morning, but there was something missing. I didn't want my career to end sitting on a circus elephant or interviewing a pastry chef.

In November 1994, I returned a call from the local mega AM station, WIBC. They were looking for a few local personalities to fill in the 9-to-12 lineup while they searched for a new host for that spot. Their list of syndicated talkers included Rush Limbaugh from 1 to 4, and while Rush was not quite the 800-pound gorilla he is now, his girth had started spreading through the talk show world by the mid-nineties.

Indiana is a conservative state. Despite having a Democratic governor at the time, Hoosiers had seldom voted for a Democrat for president. The last time was in 1966, when LBJ got the nod, ironic in this story because Johnson had been in the news that year, accused of improperly handling his beagle pups by holding them by their ears and dangling them in front of the camera. Had he done that during the election of 2004, even Indiana wouldn't have voted for him.

I doubt the general manager at WIBC saw me as a potential permanent replacement for the present host. Stan Solomon had been in that slot and was going to move to afternoon drive time. Solomon was a right-winger, always railing about Bill Clinton, convinced he murdered Vince Foster and that Hillary was femi-Nazi-lesbo. Okay, this is an exaggeration, but Solomon did attract a definite audience, just not the kind I aspired to achieve or had any chance of pleasing.

I filled in for three mornings, a total of nine hours on air—timewise the equivalent of an entire month on TV during my morning segments. It was a heady experience, but I kept the volume of the discourse turned down low. I talked about mundane issues, but I got a clear smattering of what the job would mean when one morning I expressed my opposition to corporal punishment. Listeners called, demanded I be fired, even spanked, convinced WIBC had hired a bleeding-heart liberal. Fire me? I hadn't even been hired.

Yes, I was a liberal, one of the few in Indiana, who had been given access to the airwaves. The responsibility scared the hell out of me. But it also turned me on. *Oh, please, I thought, don't ask me to do this full time. I won't be able to say no.*

Other hosts filled in the next two weeks and when I didn't hear anything for more than a month, I resigned myself to the fact that I was not right (far-right enough) for the job. I felt then, as I do now, that it is tough to offer a nuanced view of the world on the radio, which, in my opinion, is what happens when you espouse a more liberal approach to issues. But it just doesn't work. Most people need black and white, good and evil. They need something to get in a sweat about. As Garrison Keillor once noted, "Unitarian ministers don't do much preaching in the subway."

I later learned that that management had liked the reaction I had initially garnered. No one had ever disagreed with Rush. The phones had lit up. Most people didn't like what I had to say, although many did think my manner and approach were evenhanded. I was offered the job after all, with the understanding that I would present an alternative view to the right-leaning hosts presently on the air, which now included two other talkers whose shows aired in the later afternoon and evening. I was flattered by the opportunity; I didn't weigh the downside.

Mary Ellen was good at weighing. She was afraid that my decision had the potential to endanger my growing popularity at the TV station. She knew I had a penchant for looking for good issue-oriented scraps at cocktail parties, but this would take my argumentative nature to a new level. And she said it would change my brand, no doubt a concept from one of her advertising textbooks . . .

"What does that mean, 'change my brand,' Mary Ellen?"

"It means that people think they're about to take a swig of orange juice and you surprise them with grapefruit. It's jarring."

Damn, Mark Twain was right. There *is* nothing more annoying than a good example.

True, the idea of broadcasting my radical (in New York, we say enlightened) views on a 50,000-watt station throughout central Indiana did pose a risk. Maybe it did jeopardize my brand, but I was feeling my Wheaties.

My boss at WISH, Lee Giles, the news director, had heard me on the radio during the tryouts and was impressed, but his enthusiasm was tempered by concern. I was a funny guy, the reporter doing the light, fluffy stuff. And everybody enjoyed watching me (and, let's be honest, Barney), so why would I go and ruin this by actually showing people I had opinions on controversial issues? To me, it seemed as if they were afraid I'd reveal that I had a brain. Giles didn't word it that way, but that was the feeling I got.

Nevertheless, I convinced myself I had an obligation to do this: to literally broadcast a more progressive viewpoint over a radio station that was decidedly conservative. I was consumed with this feeling of self-importance. Not a flattering quality.

I took the job.

The new routine was grueling. Up at 3:30 in the morning to do my segments for Channel 8, then on to the WIBC studios by 9 AM on the north side of town to host three hours of political discourse, peppered by angry viewers who now had a good reason not to like me—despite the dog. In fact, it was not uncommon for viewers to observe that "Barney has more brains than you do."

My wife's mother, who I swear had the hots for Bill O'Reilly, considered my liberal views shameful and often denied I was her son-in-law at the retirement home bridge parties. That hurt. I wondered whether she had rewritten her will.

During all this, Barney remained my rock. Because he was with me during every morning TV segment, he also accompanied me to the radio station. We arrived each morning at about 8:30, just in time for me to review notes I had prepared at home and make a transition from my segment on TV baking chocolate éclairs or laser tag to three hours of ranting about abortion rights or gun control. There was no tougher segue in television.

In the radio studio, Barney had his own chair, actually more of a bar stool, that required some human assistance for him to negotiate. But once perched in place, he never moved the entire three hours, proof he had (1) great patience with my liberal lectures and (2) a healthy pair of kidneys.

One reason for Barney's patience—hardly a beagle trait—was that a procession of the radio staff filtered into the studio each morning, armed with a variety of dog treats. Barney sat there, unmoved (in more ways than one) by diatribes about the merits of universal health care or a harangue about prayer in school, but always with his radar set for the next person to enter the booth and slip him a nosh of pepperoni or a chocolate chip cookie.

His favorite provider was Sally, one of the veterans of the WIBC sales department who never missed a morning visit. At 10 AM sharp, just before they ran the Rush Limbaugh promo, she'd slip into the studio with a biscuit. Soon, Barney actually connected the Limbaugh theme music with her arrival. The irony never escaped me. The music got us both riled up.

I savored every minute on the air, but it had a devastating impact on me physically and emotionally. Most feedback on the air was negative, complaints about my liberal views. I thought I handled things pretty well. . . .

Caller: "I hate the government. They never do anything right. The less government, the better. We'd be better off if they would just shut down."

"What do you do for a living, sir?" I asked.

"Nothing. I'm on Social Security."

"How do you pay your medical bills?"

"I have Medicare. Oh, and I'm on disability."

"Did you go to college?"

"Yeah, on the GI Bill."

"How'd you buy your house?"

"I got an FHA loan. Say, listen, Wolfsie, what the heck does this have to do with how much I hate the government?"

The grueling part of the job was the preparation. Unlike one of the other radio hosts at the time who thought that the facts were just a distraction to his point of view, I read every newspaper and magazine. I watched every news show. I was obsessed with being totally prepared. It consumed my life, more so than the TV. I had so little time in the day to get everything done that I booked TV guests during commercial breaks on the radio.

In addition, I accepted a weekend job in New York, guest-hosting a cable show, a precursor to shows like *The Factor* and *Hannity & Colmes*. Again, a job I should have turned down. Damn ego. Now I was on TV three hours each morning, then radio the next three. The rest of the weekdays my face was either buried in a newspaper or watching news shows. Then on Friday afternoon, I'd fly to New York to do the cable show.

Brett, who was then seven, saw little of me. To Mary Ellen, I was just a rumor. It was the best year of my life. It was also the worst.

Because I was on TV every morning and because Barney was always at my side, I was a moving target with a bull's-eye on my back. Why call into the radio show when you could accost Dick Wolfsie in the supermarket or the drugstore? All of a sudden, people weren't thanking me for telling them about the new bakery in town or showing them the new museum exhibit, they were carping about my defense of the ACLU.

I was once stopped by an angry listener in a parking lot who took great issue with my views on home schooling. I listened to the guy for about ten minutes. Maybe I was just having a bad day, but for some reason I realized what a toll this radio experience was having on me.

I climbed into the car, drove about three blocks, pulled over to the side of the road, and burst into tears. I hugged Barney so hard, he squealed.

My approach on the radio didn't sell. I refused to rant. I tried to be annoyingly reasonable. But was that what the station wanted? They hoped for controversy, but they were concerned when listeners called to complain about my views. On the other hand, they knew that a strong reaction to me might ultimately generate ratings. It was an odd calculus. I was caught in the middle. Nobody knew who they wanted me to be. Least of all me, although I was sure I would not compromise my views based on viewer feedback.

Here was the bottom line (and it was all about the bottom line): You can get away with a weak opening act for Wayne Newton in Vegas. On radio, it's too easy to switch to another channel. They were beginning to think that Rush deserved a better lead-in.

Quitting did not seem like an option. I had lost enough jobs in my life that I didn't feel I had the luxury of giving one up on my own. There was hope that eventually I'd get canned. It had certainly happened before. Too many times.

After I had been on the air for about six months, a new program manager took over, part of the sale of WIBC to Emmis Communications. His last name was Hatfield, a subtle hint I was in for a feud. I knew from my first exchange with him that I was doomed. He made me justify every issue I discussed, every guest I booked, and every position I took. He didn't like the way I read the weather or the way I introduced the commercial spots. He didn't like the fact I was also on TV. Oh, and he didn't like dogs in the studio. Hey, this all looked like a fairly good clue to some serious trouble down the road.

In January 1995, I had just finished my show when I was passed a note to see the program manager immediately. I walked into his office and it was clear what would ensue. I was going to get the ax. Seated next to Hatfield was the GM, who I had thought was a decent guy and had worked with before.

"That was your last show," Hatfield said. "People don't like you. Give me your key."

Huh? I looked at the GM, who knew of my growing popularity in the TV market. The guy just sat there. Not a word. I'm still ticked about that.

Barney, who had accompanied me as always, was in the chair next to me.

"Yes, you're fired," repeated the program manager, "and so's your little dog, Barney." The wicked witch of the Midwest had spoken.

The next day, the paper ran the story of my dismissal. Later in the week, scores of letters were printed, some in support of me, but most agreeing that my views just didn't jive with most Hoosiers. I had nothing to be ashamed of, but the public nature of the axing was humiliating.

I walked out of the studio and loaded Barney in the car. I remember tilting the seat back just to rest my brain, a clear indication to the beagle that he could nestle his head on my lap. This was common behavior when we went on speaking engagements that required a lengthy road trip and a nap along the way at a rest stop.

I have no romantic notions that dogs always sense what their owner is feeling. I only know this: With his face in my lap, he rolled his eyes toward the top of his head and fixed his gaze on me. When I finally returned the seat to the upright position, his head remained in my lap for the trip home.

For me, it was the end of daily hourlong debates about O. J. Simpson, Bosnia, and welfare mothers. For Barney, it was the end of 10 AM treats. We would both survive. We had a TV show to do the next morning.

Mary Ellen was relieved, and not surprised at the news. She thought Brett would benefit from the change. That night I decided to tell my son, couching it in a positive narrative. "Dad has some great news. You know how little time we have to spend together? Well, starting tomorrow, Dad has decided not to do the radio show anymore. I want to have more time for us to fish together, read stories, and play baseball." Brett, whose nose was buried in a plate of SpaghettiOs, glanced at my wife and said, "Hey, Mom, I think Dad got fired!"

The next day I was free of that daunting responsibility of reading all the *New York Times* editorials and every article in *Newsweek,* and gagging through Rush's show on the way home in the car.

It was fine with Barney, I thought. The chair was really not very comfortable in the studio. There were plenty of treats at home. Home. That had a nice sound to it.

A few months after my dismissal at the radio station, Sally, the sales rep who had so loved Barney and supplied him with daily treats, was diagnosed with cancer. During her illness, Barney and I visited her at home and on several occasions and when she felt up to it, she would show up at one of our morning segments. Barney recognized her perfume and would howl at the top of his lungs when she was within one hundred feet.

On one occasion, we went to the hospital to see Sally, but we were stopped at the elevator by a security guard who gave Barney the once-over. "Is he a service dog?"

"No."

"Is he a therapy dog?"

"No, this is Barney from Channel 8," I explained.

"Go right in," said the guard, who broke into a huge grin. He had known it all along. Within five minutes, every nurse on the floor and several patients came to meet Barney.

Sally died six months later.

At the funeral, her best friend, Margo, asked if I had a photo of Barney in my car. When I retrieved the picture, she motioned me to accompany her to the open coffin. When we approached, Margo slipped the photo under Sally's folded arms. "I think Sally would have wanted this. She sure loved Barney."

This felt like a kind of closure to the radio experience, bittersweet though, it was. I don't have many fond memories of my time on the radio, except I was happy that Barney had touched Sally's life. That seemed to make it all worthwhile. But what would you expect a bleeding-heart liberal like me to say?

The Reality of Television

Many people who might have been reluctant to appear on TV were more open to the idea knowing that Barney was part of the mix. My favorite story is about Jerry Hostetler, then about sixty, and owner of the most garish house in town. His 55,000-square-foot home could have been charitably described as Vegas Gauche.

The modular structure had about fifty rooms, but that was just a guess because you really didn't know when one room ended and the next began. The house was filled—but not decorated—with priceless antiques and works of art from around the world. Despite the value of his collection, the inside looked like a garage sale.

There were a dozen workmen on the premises 24/7, bowing to every whim Jerry had on any given day about the house. "Let's move the bathroom over there," he'd tell a plumber, who never flinched. Why would he? He was being paid by the hour. The entire facility was a work in progress. If you could call it progress.

People in cars were always lined up on the street to see the house, which featured huge stone dolphin statues spouting water into a fountain on the front circle drive. Part of the allure was Jerry's past, which was probably a bit shady, but it always got shadier in the retelling. He was in the restoration business, so after a flood or fire, Jerry would haggle with the insurance companies over how much they would pay their clients. Jerry did very well at this. Too well, some thought, considering his house and furnishings.

But no one had ever done a story about the house because there were rumors he did not talk to reporters. He even shot at one, I had heard.

I was sure that wasn't true, but for years I had driven past the house, lacking the nerve to knock on the door. One day, Barney by my side, I took the plunge and pulled into his driveway. "Is Mr. Hostetler here?" I asked a gardener working on the front lawn. "Can I see him?"

"He's in the garage getting a manicure."

Sure enough, there he was, decked out in a, well, deck chair—a beautiful Hispanic woman attending to his hair and nails next to one of his three Jaguar XKEs. I felt like I was meeting Howard Hughes.

Jerry was more than cordial, even self-effacing, admitting that he had heard the rumors about himself and assured me that *most* were not true. He even admitted to watching Barney and me on TV in the mornings, *before* he went to bed. As George Carlin once said, "The sixties were good to this guy."

His good mood turned a bit sour when I requested permission to do a TV show about his unique dwelling. That temporarily ended the conversation, but he did assure me he would think about it and said I should call his secretary the next week.

When I called Carol, his assistant, she told me that Jerry

wanted to make me an offer, which scared the hell out of me, but I listened. "You can do a show at Jerry's home, if he can hire someone to snap pictures of him and Barney together throughout the house."

And so it was. Barney and I arrived two weeks later, greeted by Jerry's personal public relations man and a professional photographer. That's when we did the first live remote from the legendary residence. Barney had free run of the house and in one memorable shot, Barney was seen waddling down the wrought iron spiral staircase that led from one of the second-story party rooms to the living room on the main floor. Scarlett O'Hara, eat your heart out.

Jerry got his photos and I got my TV interview and tour.

Jerry died a few years after that. His house—considered by neighbors an eyesore—went unsold for quite a while, but it is now the property of a young dot-com millionaire, new to town. When I had the occasion to meet the thirty-year-old owner, I told him the story I have recounted above.

"Who's Barney, again?" he asked.

Who, indeed!

Some people, like Jerry, may fear being on television. I have always said that there are two types of people: those who would do *anything* to get on TV, and those who would do *anything* to avoid it.

Here's some good advice for both groups:

Being on TV frightens people to death. In some ways it is scarier than public speaking. Of course, in a way, it is public speaking, but a camera seems even more threatening than a roomful of people.

When I arrived at a remote spot for Channel 8, I would request that everyone who didn't want to be on TV gather in a specific corner. Once the masses grouped to avoid media exposure, I began the segment by having my cameraman zoom in on all the huddlers who "didn't want to be seen on TV." This caused a kind of mass hysteria, especially women who had arisen at 4:30 in the morning to bring their kids to the show and had skipped the makeup portion of their morning ritual. There was a lot of high-pitched screaming, back-turning, and huddling. Most were good-natured about it. Not all, but most.

It is really the talking on TV, not the being on TV, that petrifies everyone—a fear of making a fool of yourself, saying something really dumb.

Case in point: In 1997, a nurse at the medical clinic at Indianapolis Motor Speedway was panicked about being *live* on the air to discuss how the ER treated race drivers who were hurt in collisions. I assured her that she was the expert and if she just relaxed she would be fine. I even told her what the first question would be.

"So, tell the viewers," I asked during first segment, "what is the first thing you do if a driver is admitted to the ER with a head injury?"

"I'd take off his pants," she said.

I think she was a bit nervous. Or a very friendly nurse.

Of course, now with YouTube and reality TV, there's a whole new generation of the public convinced that the dumber you appear on the screen or in a video, the greater the chances of being seen nationally and becoming a star or at least a topic of national conversation.

Back in the nineties, I happily capitalized on a goof with self-deprecation, calling attention to the misstep. Reporters with breaking news stories don't have this luxury. Even today, serious journalists don't want a YouTube moment if it compromises their professionalism.

Dealing with an individual's trepidation about being

interviewed on TV is a responsibility I take seriously. Many of my guests have never been on TV or have had an unpleasant experience: a host who was not prepared, or asked bizarre questions, was distant or uninterested.

Barney truly made a difference in the minutes before an interview. Those who might have otherwise been total wrecks seemed to calm down a touch if they first interacted with Barney. While Barney's modus operandi usually involved sniffing his surroundings when we first arrived, he would ultimately come over to greet the guest and give a friendly wag. I wished he could have gone over some of the questions I was going to ask, but that was my job. Giving a guest—especially one new to TV—some idea of what the interview is about goes a long way toward making the experience less stressful. Unless it's an adversarial interview where your intent is to play gotcha, there is no excuse for the reporter not helping to prepare the interviewee. In my opinion, too many reporters and talk show hosts don't do this.

Having interviewed over 25,000 people in the past three decades, I do have tips for those who may someday find themselves on TV.

If you are reading this and have a memo on your desk to return a call to *60 Minutes'* Mike Wallace, forget this last paragraph and seek legal help. If you have something to hide, my tips will not help you. If you have clean hands, call Mike Wallace back.

Here are some things to remember—the three As.

Attitude: Being interviewed is not brain surgery, although if you have an MD or a PhD in neuroscience, the interview might be *about* brain surgery. You know more about your topic than the reporter or host, no matter how prepared he or she is—which is why you have been invited on the show to begin with. You are the resident expert on your topic, so relax and feel confident.

Answers: You are in control. No matter what you are asked, there are ways to get in the information you want to convey. Decide on a few things you want to say, a few points you want to make, and practice giving them in short, informative sentences. If you are truly not trying to hide anything and your answer is entertaining and informative, your interviewer will be happy.

Suppose, for example, that you have written a book about your travels around the world. Your favorite story is how you taught a polar bear at the North Pole to play the violin.

Q. So, Mr. Lewis, I understand you've been to the South Pole.

A. Yes, and it was glorious, but nothing compared to my incredible experience at the North Pole with a polar bear.

If the interviewer still wants to know about the South Pole after that, he's an idiot. Unless, of course, he has substantial evidence that you ran an illegal dog-sled operation at the South Pole.

Attire: Earth colors are best. Avoid black and white, which tend to wash out your face. Most people wear the right colors by sheer chance, so unless you are Zorro, a nun, or a member of the KKK, you'll be fine.

Men should always wear long socks. Even George Clooney has an ugly lower leg. No hats, dangling-jewelry overload, or chewing gum. These don't apply if you are there to talk about the return of the derby, sell cheap jewelry, or represent the short-sock fan club, but there is no excuse for gum. Also, ladies should not wear extra makeup and men will generally be given a little powder for the forehead if the interview is in-studio. If you sweat profusely because you're nervous, read this article ten times before doing the show. If you're completely bald, you will still look bald on TV.

If you're going on a talk show, get to the studio at least an hour early. Chances are, the producers will put you in a waiting area called a green room. In the green room (which is never green), you will have a chance to talk to other guests. If you discover that the host is a jerk, that his goal is to embarrass his guests, and that he has a horrible reputation for not keeping his word, you will then have time to sneak out.

In most cases, a producer will visit you in the green room. Tell the producer what you want to talk about. She or he will share this with the host. Some hosts will come by themselves and speak to you in person, but many think this ruins the spontaneity of the show. Bull! I've done it for thirty years. If your interview is of a personal nature, request, even demand, a short chat with the host beforehand. If you are being interviewed by a street reporter, still make an attempt for a personal conversation first. Again, some reporters and hosts won't do this, though it's sometimes an issue of time rather than preference.

Finally, some showtime tips:

Sit up: Most couches on sets are very soft. Once in Columbus, Ohio, we lost a guest in a beige couch for three days. Sitting up straight exudes an air of confidence. Don't slouch. If there's a fire alarm, two hundred thousand viewers will be watching you struggle to get up. Not pretty.

Speak up: The key to confidence is not to mumble. You will scare yourself to death if you whisper. Listen to the host's or reporter's voice. He may be a jerk, but he usually knows how loudly to speak.

Look up: Look at the host. Do not look at the camera. I am always amazed that reporters and hosts don't mention this to the guest. I've forgotten myself.

Avoid jargon: Change the pitch and tone of your voice to make a point. Talk pretty much the way you might in regular conversation. Don't be afraid to use your hands.

In summary, show passion. If you do not communicate that you had fun at the North Pole, no one will care how many polar bears you trained to play the violin. Success is all about sharing your enthusiasm.

Last but not least, be yourself. Unless "yourself" is a boring, aloof, self-centered, pompous egotist. But, of course, by definition, if that were you, you wouldn't be aware of it.

Once the interview is over, you may feel you mumbled, looked nervous, and said really stupid things. Watch the tape, and assuming your VCR or DVR was set correctly, you'll see it wasn't nearly that bad. If, however, you think you were the greatest and are considering writing to Oprah to be her fill-in guest host, it probably wasn't that good either.

If you videotaped *Girls Gone Wild* by mistake instead of the show where you talked about your new solar panels, give the station a call and ask for a copy of the interview on a DVD. They will be glad to help. For $129.95.

During my almost thirty years on TV, people frequently requested a copy of their interviews on VHS or DVD, often an indication that even in this high-tech age, people were still clueless when it came to recording segments off the air. Nothing has changed.

"I tried to TiVo the show, Dick, but I got *Jerry Springer* instead."

One thing was certain during the nineties: If guests had any interaction at all with Barney during the morning program, the chances they would want a copy of the show increased dramatically. Barney changed the experience from an interview into an event.

The classic Barney photo by Ed Bowers. We printed 5,000 of them and signed each one to fans: Your pals, Dick and Barney.

Executives substitute Barney's photo for the morning anchor's on WISH-TV's wall of fame.

At a local hotel. Barney gave it four stars—mostly for the room service.

The sign might have said "NO PETS" but Barney was a fan of NO RULES. He was at home everywhere.

At the Fair. If it moved, he chased it. If it didn't, he ate it.

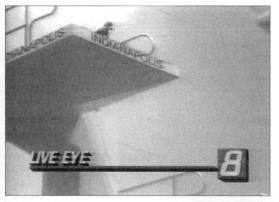

On top of a diving platform at the local natatorium. He didn't jump, but all of Indiana held their breath.

Barney jazzes it up at a local club. He was always ready to party.

At the second annual Barney Look-alike contest. Even the Bull-dog won a prize.

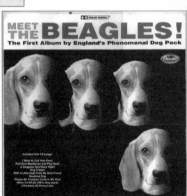

With a little help from my (best) friend. There was only one Barney. That was enough.

Playing to a special audience. Barney spends the morning with children who have Down Syndrome.

Barney gets his own TV show (top).

He once slept through *Lassie Come Home* (left).

Time to go home. Where's the limo? (bottom)

Barney and I promote a local movie theater.

Hey, leave that popcorn alone!

Sorry, I forgot the butter.

With the Girl Scouts promoting the American Dairy Association.
Always a trooper.

Emily Hunt had been
paralyzed in a tragic
accident, but Barney
always brightened her
spirits.

My first interview after Barney's death. I said there would never be another Barney. And I was right.

The doctors in this clinic never treated Barney. They just loved him like everyone else.

The Story in Brief(s)

I felt early on as I watched people's reactions to Barney that his true mission was to touch lives, just as he had touched Sally's from WIBC. When people saw Barney in person their moods visibly altered. Barney didn't care if you had just come from the symphony or the silo. Whether you smelled of money or manure, he was your buddy. Sure, all dogs are like that, but not all dogs were Barney. He was on TV. You had met a celebrity.

Barney was all heart and howl but not much of a businessman. He needed me to look out for the best opportunities to maximize his potential. I saw every would-be guest for the show through a kind of beagle lens. How could I work Barney into the segment? That was not the only criterion, but when things were in the balance, that could tip the scale. Like the time a local sign-maker wanted to publicize a new apparatus he had purchased that could inexpensively produce refrigerator magnets with a photo of your choice embossed on it.

Making a magnet with Barney's face on it would be good TV. Everybody would want one. *So,* I thought, *let's offer a free magnet to anybody who simply sent a self-addressed stamped envelope to his shop.* I told the owner my idea.

"Say what, now?" he said. Yes, I got that response a lot.

But wait, I had an even a better idea. How about two magnets: one with Barney's mug on it and one with Dave Barras's, our morning anchor. You could have only one. So which one would you request in the mail? How diabolical!

I didn't tell Dave I was going to do this, which you can look at as a testimony to what a good-natured, unaffected, self-assured guy he was to work with. You could also just say I was a big jerk because it was clear that in this man-to-mongrel contest, Dave was going to get hammered.

The morning of the show, we displayed the two magnets on the air, both having been previously designed from a photo of Barney I had given the sign shop and an eight-by-ten glossy of Dave I had stolen from the cache of PR material in his desk. Dave had always boasted that his photos were in such great demand that there was a six-month wait before his staff could fill a request. Not true, but a funny refrain he used on the air for many years.

Remember in the movie *Miracle on 34th Street,* when bags of letters addressed to Santa Claus are delivered to the courthouse? The next two days at the 'ol sign shop looked much the same as that scene in the Christmas classic. Requests for the magnet kept pouring in. How many self-addressed stamped envelopes were delivered? About three thousand in two days.

I thought I would have a happy magnet maker, but he and I were poles apart in terms of what success meant. For three weeks the guy complained to me about the extra help he had to hire to stuff envelopes. Then he discovered that the postage we requested was not enough to mail the magnet. Then angry people who got Dave's magnet by mistake started to call. It was getting ugly out there.

What were the final numbers? I will not give you the exact stats out of respect for my buddy Dave. Despite his claim on the air that day, he apparently did not have a magnetic personality. But in one way, Dave has saved face after all these years, even though so few wanted his face. His magnets are probably worth much more today than Barney's. But that's because they were so rare.

Not a week goes by that people don't boast that they still have a Barney magnet on their fridge. What a testimony. There's Barney next to kids, grandkids, and family recipes on the appliance door. People see Barney every day, just before they indulge in a forbidden snack. Barney would have appreciated the appropriate use of his image. Can you think of a better example of product placement?

I did come up with one. It began with a phone call from a local clothing manufacturer. He was looking for some promotion for his sports apparel business that produced a line of made-to-order clothing featuring team logos and school names.

The guy was asking me for some free publicity, which was not an uncommon request. The sales department adored Barney. They also enjoyed being in the black financially and were seldom happy when a TV segment could potentially have been a paid ad. I always felt that in some way everybody was "selling" something. So it was hard to distinguish between hawking a product and those just spreading a point of view.

If the sales manager questioned why I had booked a certain segment, I often made the case that being on *Daybreak* might convince a potential advertiser of the power of television because inevitably those few minutes on the air with me and Barney led to company recognition and business. That would result in a greater chance the guy would become a client and cough up a few bucks. That was the tune I sang my entire career. This particular request, however, did seem to cross the line. A visit to a facility where people manufactured shorts and T-shirts just wasn't good TV.

With this in mind, I politely explained the problem with doing the segment. Just as I was about to hang up, the proverbial lightbulb went on. There was a way to make it good TV.

"Tell you what," I said to the owner. "I'll do a show about your company if you'll agree to make a line of underwear with Barney's picture plastered all over each pair."

"Are you serious?"

With that ringing endorsement, I convinced him this would be a great promotion. The shorts would be priced inexpensively so our viewers would order on impulse. We'd call them Beagle Boxers. (Boxers! Get it? Like the breed of dog.) And we'd take phone orders during the show.

He was hesitant, concerned that too many sales at the price we agreed on (ten bucks) would mess up waiting orders for other clients, especially because the boxers required labor-intensive stitching. I comforted him. "Don't worry. We couldn't possibly sell that many. I mean, what man would want a beagle on his underwear?" Somehow, I never felt guilty when I shaded the truth. My gut told me this was a great idea.

Three weeks later, we did a show from his plant, explaining how the Barney boxers had gone from design to production. We displayed the original concept on the computer, then showed his seamstresses and tailors in action completing each pair at their sewing machines. The whole setting had a kind of sweatshop look to it, which concerned me, but as was often the case with live TV, once you're there you have to make the best of it.

The shorts completed, we wrestled a pair on Barney. This had to be the most humiliated he had ever been. He didn't howl at me for a week. But Barney was always a good sport about wearing stuff: hats, shoes, scarves, earmuffs. Over the years he had a Santa suit and even a Harley biker outfit, both made just for dogs. The only thing he resisted wearing were those silly reindeer antlers. He did have some sense of style.

As soon as we mentioned on camera that the shorts were for sale, the switchboard was slammed. Even with the extra personnel the owner had hired, his staff couldn't keep up. To his credit, he knew he could not cut off the calls at the agreed time, so we extended the hours viewers could order. "I'll take calls until noon," he relented. I have never seen a man so unhappy selling underwear.

By noon, over 1,000 pairs of shorts had been sold. His employees, who assembled the boxers by hand, worked overtime the next two weeks filling the orders for Father's Day, an upcoming date I had conveniently forgotten to remind the owner of. As it turned out, I was correct when I said that most men would not want beagle underwear. However, a lot of women did want to buy their husbands beagle underwear, whether they wanted a pair or not. Let that be a lesson to all of you going into sales and marketing.

Rumor has it that there was a minor baby boom nine months after the shorts were delivered. Not true, but it's the only reference to sex in this entire book. To this day, at fairs and book signings, men tell me that they still have their pair of Barney Boxers. Once a guy said he was wearing them. I took his word for it.

Concerto for Four Paws

There is no real magic bullet when it comes to advertising. Even Super Bowl ads, despite the huge investment, have come up short. The research is clear: Just because you remember an ad doesn't mean you will buy the product. Or even remember what product the ad was touting. Being from Indianapolis, I love that ad with Peyton Manning for . . . for . . . not a clue. See what I mean?

Up until Barney arrived on the scene, I had never done a TV commercial. Not one. First, I was technically a newsperson both at the NBC and CBS affiliate. As a rule, reporters don't have the luxury of extra income in this area. It poses a conflict of interest. Suppose Katie Couric did a spot for Carnival Cruise Lines and a bad batch of calamari wiped out the entire early seating. That puts Katie in a very awkward spot that evening reporting the news.

Barney changed the rules. We were both for sale.

The first gig came out of my middle-age crisis. I had wanted a motorcycle, but my wife said I could take piano lessons instead.

We compromised and I took the piano lessons. I signed up with a well-known instructor at a music showroom up the street from the station. It was always mortifying to sit outside the teacher's studio waiting my turn only to hear a well-rehearsed seven-year-old playing a Mozart concerto. I also knew full well that the seven-year-old who followed me would have to listen to my rendition of "Born Free" for a fifth consecutive week.

Barney accompanied me on every lesson, trying to snooze in the corner of the room. Whenever I played, I imagined the scene from *Our Gang* comedies when Butch, the black-eyed mongrel, would cover his ears and eyes with his paws when there was an unpleasant stimulus.

After several months, I could play "Born Free" and maybe two other songs, but the owner of the store thought it was cool that Dick and Barney were at his studio taking lessons. And so, the first print ad was born, a photo of Barney and me on the piano stool with the tag: "If Barney and Dick can learn to play the Clavinova, anyone can." The ad was a hit.

Requests for Barney (and me) to do personal appearances started to climb—even from corporations that had local ties to Indy but were headquartered elsewhere. This often led to some confusion. . . .

"Hello, may I speak to Barney Wolfsie?"

"Excuse me?"

"This is Cal Larson from CVS Pharmacy in Minneapolis. I'd like to talk with Barney Wolfsie, please."

"Yes, he's here, but look, he's a dog. Do you still want to talk to him?"

(Long, *long* pause.) "You say he's a dog? There must be some mistake."

"Well, I don't know whose mistake it would be. We both feel pretty good about the whole arrangement," I'd reply.

(Another long pause.) "This is CVS Corporate and we're opening a new store in Indy. The store manager has a budget for a local celebrity to appear and he gave us Barney Wolfsie's name."

"Well, this is Dick Wolfsie."

"Do you work for your brother?"

No matter what I said, it didn't seem to sink in, like I was talking to an Irish setter. He wouldn't let go. "Hmmm. Does Barney make personal appearances?"

"That's the only kind he makes!" I said.

"I see. Would he be available on August 18 at around 2 PM?" CVS Corporate was not taking "no" for an answer.

"Let me check my calendar. Yes, we're available."

(Another pause.) "Oh, do you go with him?"

I explained the situation again, and again, and again. I thought I had finally made it clear. Barney and I made our appearance that summer. We stood in the doorway and greeted customers. Many had indeed come by to meet us in person. Although, based on the age of the turnout, the sale on Depends might have been the bigger draw.

When I received the check from CVS Corporate, you guessed it: it was made out to Barney Wolfsie. The next day at the bank, I anticipated trouble. Barney still had a hell of a time using a ballpoint pen and we had never opened an account for him, despite his ample income. I put Barney's paw print on the back and countersigned it, and the nice people at Bank One cashed it for us.

Contract Sports

Every year or so, depending on the length of my contract at Channel 8, it was time to see how much more money I could squeeze out of my employer.

I would nervously walk into News Director Lee Giles's office and edge into my seat in front of his desk. At that point, Barney would hop into the chair next to me, sitting straight up in his seat. Barney never snoozed during these discussions. I don't think he trusted me. I was kind of a pushover in this area.

I liked the fact that Barney was with me because he was a visual reminder that I brought to the table something different—a shtick no other reporter had. And Barney always liked being brought to the table. The week before the meeting, he'd made his contribution to the cause during an early morning snowstorm. Luckily, that day Giles was in the control room.

This was generally a bit early for the blue suits to be at the station, but bad weather meant huge ratings. Even non–TV viewers gravitated to the screen for school closings and driving conditions, so our coverage of the inclement weather could be used to attract new watchers and distinguish ourselves from the competition.

Dick Wolfsie

During my segment, I tried to give a sense of what the situation would be like for commuters. On this particular morning, snow had drifted several feet in spots, and I was standing knee deep in a pile of white stuff to demonstrate its depth. Suddenly, I heard Giles screaming in my ear from the control room. "Where's Barney? Show how deep the snow is compared to a beagle." I am confident this was the first time in TV history these words were ever uttered by a news director.

Barney, who had been trudging along sniffing the snow like a pig searching for truffles, plowed chest first into a drift. The snow was up to his neck, his head now poking out, his nose twitching like a man smelling bad fish.

"Perfect," said a gleeful Giles, in love with his last-minute decision to use Barney as a yardstick for people deciding whether to don galoshes or chance it with loafers. Once the segment ended, Barney retreated to the car and barked to get back inside.

Lee was right. The next day in the supermarket, a procession of people in line to buy salt and snow shovels asked if Barney had survived his ordeal, and a few who had not seen him in later segments were a little concerned he had been lost in the drifting accumulations.

Barney was not lost in the drifts, nor did his appearance—albeit requested by the boss himself—wind up making me a wealthier man. I never got more than a 4 percent annual raise the entire time I worked with Barney. This will probably raise the hackles of some of my colleagues who maybe got 3 percent, but all this speaks to a common misconception about TV salaries. While it's true that longtime anchors and occasionally talent lured from another market can garner bigger salaries, as a general rule, your run-of-the-town general assignment reporter will never get rich.

I had no agent because I always felt that at my relatively low level I would just be giving back whatever extra bucks the guy whittled out of WISH. To bargain effectively you have to be irreplaceable (and no one is) or have a very distorted view of your importance (which everybody does).

So, given that I had this incredible sidekick, why didn't I feel irreplaceable? Why didn't I slam my fist on the desk and tell WISH to take a walk when the offer was so low? Mainly because I felt they would simply tell me to take a walk—and take my dog with me. That would have been okay with Barney. Walking was his favorite thing. Next to being brought to the table.

The truth is that the pairing of my name with the dog was clearly positive for my career, but I also knew that the twist of fate that had brought us together carried some risks. Not only could the dog get old and die, but so could the act. I don't think that anyone—certainly not me—would have predicted a twelve-year run, so it was hard to really use the dog as a bargaining chip. I felt pretty good about my ability on camera, but assigning part of my success to Barney was self-defeating, maybe even demeaning. How would I play it? Ultimately, I let the boss do all the talking. I never boasted in the contract negotiations how popular the dog had made the show. That seemed a dangerous road to go down. But I knew he had made a huge difference.

And Lee Giles knew it. In fact, he was once quoted as saying, "That dog just has natural instincts for TV. That's more than I can say for some reporters." (I asked for a detailed list of those he was talking about but he declined the request.)

During the discussions, Barney was always with me. He just sat upright in the chair next to mine. Lee recalls that

Barney would just stare at him, maybe daring him to go below 3 percent.

When we were done settling the contract, all three of us would shake hands. My partner and I would then walk out the door. Barney's eyes would migrate to the top of his head and roll around as if to say: "You call that negotiating? You rolled over like a well-behaved dog."

"Fine, Barney, next time you do all the talking."

Showing His True Spots

Soon enough, Barney became an integral part of the news, featured almost every day in one form or another in my segment each morning, but he had failed to clear one hurdle that was a true indicator of his value. The station had not run any promotional spots that featured him, nor had he been included in the news opening when the other anchors and talent were highlighted.

I hesitated to push for this. News talent is notorious for feeling left out of station promotions. "Promote me, promote me" is a common request, though the approach is sometimes more subtle. Authors are no different. "Why isn't my book about Barney displayed more prominently?" I'll ask the store manager. Ego, ego, ego. Imagine that.

But I felt I had a good case. Barney created water-cooler talk, a very unscientific but accurate predictor of a show's popularity. Every TV producer with a few years under his or her belt knows that chatter the next day can turn into ratings. My sense was always that this was less true of hard news than the regular network programming, but that is exactly why

Barney was so important. He made our news presentation totally unique.

It was unlikely, for example, that people at the Chrysler assembly plant would talk about the bank robbery they heard about on TV the night before, unless it was the bank next door. If they did chat about it, it was not always true they could identify the station they were watching. Similar coverage was usually on all the affiliates and it's hard to connect a particular story with a specific news organization unless you are a very loyal viewer. There are only so many ways to cover a story. True, I always thought we did a better job, but a bank robbery is still a bank robbery.

One method of separating yourself from other shops (TV lingo for news competitors) is with your talent, the people who do the news. But only a small percentage of TV news personalities break through and are connected by the public to a station on the proverbial—but now extinct—dial. What you want to do is build that core audience. But just like in politics, there are independents—folks who are not committed and will go wherever the mood—and the remote—takes them.

This is where Barney showed his tri-colors. "What makes people good on TV is acting natural," Giles commented. "And Barney *was* a natural. He was just Barney, and it was fun having him around when the news wasn't too serious."

After a Barney segment, people talked about it, laughed about it, and identified him with WISH-TV. So with that in mind, the promotion people at the station finally made the next bold move. They not only wanted Barney in the news open, but they wanted to feature him in a station promotion that would air throughout the day.

Rather than being taped at the TV studio, this spot was going to be outsourced to a local video production facility, a big deal because when you go out of house with an ad campaign, it costs extra and your expectations are higher because of the increased production value.

A day before the shoot was scheduled, I received a script from the promotion director, Scott Hainey. I knew Dean Crowe, the videographer we were using; he was a real pro but not known for his patience. Not really a problem, except that the draft of the script was heavily dependent on Barney's cooperation in a rather complex scenario where the anchors, Dave and Pam, and our meteorologist, Randy, along with Barney and me, would play musical chairs. The idea was for Barney to jump onto the remaining seat each time the music stopped, leaving only Barney in a chair at the end of the commercial spot.

Sure, and I also wanted Barney to get up early and cook me breakfast every morning. It wasn't going to happen.

"Yeah, yeah, very funny," Crowe grumbled when he saw the layout of the spot. "I hope I'm home in time for Christmas." (It was October.)

I didn't blame him for being skeptical. Whoever wrote the ad had a great idea, but just because it looked good on paper didn't mean we could pull it off. Dogs don't know how to play musical chairs. Do they?

Dean had not only underestimated the brilliant theatrical abilities of my dog, he had forgotten the persuasive effect of a hunk of pepperoni. Each time we did a take, the lead anchor cupped a piece of the succulent treat in his hand. Barney kept in close proximity as the Channel 8 talent paraded around the chairs. When the music stopped, everyone sat down, but the anchors always left an open seat next to the pepperoni purveyor. Barney never missed a cue. As soon as the chair opened up, Barney jumped into it, hoping for an opportunity to make a major taste-bud score.

We did twenty or thirty takes, but few, if any, of those retakes resulted from Barney's failure to perform on cue. It was usually one of the camera crew who had missed a shot or one of the anchors who had blown a line or tripped over a chair.

When we left, about an hour ahead of schedule, Dean Crowe just shook his head. "I love working with animals," he laughed. "They're so much smarter than television people."

The ad was a success. For months people asked how I got Barney to do that. The secret was in the pepperoni and Barney's experience that an empty chair was an invitation to rest and maybe earn a treat. In Barney's case, a dry biscuit would have fallen short. We had to bring out the good stuff.

His Station in Life

Along the way, there were various signposts that Barney had arrived: He was in promotional ads; he was doing commercials; he had his own show, *Barney's Bad Movies*; he had more air time than most reporters. What was left? What other indicator would clearly demonstrate that Barney was no flash in the pan?

During one remote in the mid-nineties I was on a shoot where several other stations were also broadcasting. I always strived to book segments that were not generally considered traditional news. As a result, it was rare that we would find ourselves in the same venue.

In cases where more than one station is at the same locale, the TV crews have to jockey times and be flexible so that each affiliate has a shot at the guest and no one misses out. While stations are competitive, early morning news people are cooperative so that everyone can get the sound bite or video needed.

One year at the Christmas auto extravaganza at what was then the RCA Dome, photographers were whipping their cameras around, taping the prototype cars, and searching for experts who were roaming the show in preparation for the door-opening later in the morning.

Reporters wear earpieces called IFBs, which stands for Interruptible Feedback, something even I didn't know for almost twenty years. I do know this: it is the lifeline back to the studio, allowing the producer to communicate to the newsperson in the field, providing time cues and input on the segment. They are notoriously unreliable, sometimes too loud, occasionally too soft, and often they don't work at all. If you are a careful observer, you will occasionally see a reporter yank the plug out of his ear, usually an indication that a technical snafu has resulted in what's called a mix-minus. Translation: You hear what you just said a second after you said it. It's not just annoying, it's virtually impossible to communicate with that kind of feedback in your ear. You are reduced to a bumbling idiot. More so than usual.

That particular morning, Barney was in rare form. We had just shot a commercial with him and he was enjoying his freedom to dash among the new cars, greeting the cleanup crew and early guests who had arrived for interviews. He did make a point of leaving his calling card on a few tires. Barney rarely had an accident, but in all fairness, what the heck was a car doing inside a building?

I was apologizing to the maintenance staff when I saw a fellow newsman from another station yank the IFB out of his ear. His producer wasn't happy and was sharing those feelings. The reporter had a huge grin on his face and motioned me to walk over to him. He held the IFB up near *my* ear so I could hear what was being said.

"We can't use any of that video later in the morning," he shouted. "That damn Channel 8 dog is in every shot. They will cook my ass and yours when they see that. Move the camera. I don't even want to see his tail wagging."

Quite a statement. TV stations never give any air time, even a mention, of a competitor's on-air personalities. Similarly, camera crews assiduously avoid even having the briefest shot of another station's vehicle, a boldly colored advertisement for the company. But a dog's tail. That seemed overly paranoid.

The more Barney appeared on TV, the more he became a household word, the more wanna-be guests realized that the way to my heart was through my beagle. It had reached the point where many requests to be on the show were couched in some reference to Barney and how he could be included in the segment. Guests also knew that not only did a Barney tie-in increase their chances that I would be receptive to booking them, but the segment would have additional marketing pay-off for them. So even if it wasn't the guest's idea, they jumped when I made the suggestion to include Barney in some way.

Willow Marketing, a downtown Indy marketing and PR agency, had a really nifty promotional idea. They were looking for the worst, that's right, the *worst* corporate logo in the Indianapolis market. Once it was determined, they would create a new logo for the "lucky winner," and profits for that company would then soar. Or maybe they wouldn't soar. But who cared? It was a great idea for a promotion. I liked the way they were thinking. Then I started thinking.

"Tell you what I'll do," I told Brad, the president of the company. "Let's create a logo for Barney that I can use when Barney makes commercials. We'll show the creative process on TV. It would help promote your contest."

"So, Dick, you want my company to make a free logo for your dog, so you can then market your dog and make money? That sounds awfully self-serving, self-indulgent, and self-promotional."

This guy caught on fast. But he knew it made sense. Barney was a star and a franchise. But what's a franchise without a logo? What's a tin man without a heart? A scarecrow without a brain? You get the point. Every dog has his day, but not every dog has his own logo. Once again, Barney would become one of the exceptions.

Brad's staff drew up several ideas and during one of our TV spots we sat with the creative group while they discussed each artist's renditions—the pros and cons of each logo. They were not haphazardly slapped together. Some honest market research had gone into their designs and production and there was a serious discussion about each option and its chances of success. "Do we want to stress his cuteness or his intelligence? Do we want the logo to reflect his independent nature or his loyalty? Should it just be 'Barney' or 'Barney the Beagle'?" Huh? I had never considered stuff like that. For me, it was a crash course in marketing and design. And having a logo paid off.

All twelve logos were shown on TV and the viewers voted for their favorite. They chose my top pick, a caricature profile of the celebrity dog donning some very cool sunglasses. People said he looked like Snoopy, who, I've been told, was another famous beagle. Sorry, never heard of him.

The winning design was so cool that a local Toyota dealership agreed to lease me a car at no cost if I would put the Barney logo on selected spots on the automobile. When I told Mary Ellen, she rolled her eyes, suggesting it would look cheesy. When I told her that it would save us about $10,000 over the next three years, she became a little more lactose tolerant.

That same dealership used Barney for several of their own spots, including one where he appears to be driving one of their top-selling models. We propped his paws up on the steering wheel. It was very funny, but apparently too realistic. The station received e-mails from people concerned that

Barney was not wearing a seat belt. So I guess it was okay that a dog was driving a car. As long as he was buckled up.

All over Indianapolis, things were named after Barney. And a few still remain. There's a special place at a local kennel called Barney's Suite Retreat. Pet owners frequently request that space. A sandwich at a local deli was named after Barney. It was all meat, no bun. At one local eatery, Barney even had his own mini wine cellar. At the Humane Society, a dog log cabin bore his name for several years. Dozens of people named their dogs—and cats—after Barney. No children, as far as I know.

But what would be the greatest testament possible to any canine? How about a drink named after him at one of the top steak houses in America: Ruth's Chris. Think of the honor. Patrons sip a very special libation bearing his name, before sinking their teeth into a $35 hunk of heaven.

No dog would turn his nose up at that opportunity. Except maybe a French poodle.

Now, Barney had already had one misadventure at Ruth's Chris. Years earlier, Ruth Fertel, whose name the restaurant bears, came to Indy to open a new franchise. She was a dog lover and had heard about Barney through her local contacts. I planned a show at the new location. Her PR person requested I bring Barney with me, but I argued that this was a bad idea. Technically speaking, I was not supposed to bring Barney into a restaurant because it violated the health code. However, I had often ignored that rule and had never been questioned.

In any case, Ruth's PR person was adamant that Barney come along. When I arrived, I initially left him in the car, but then Ruth insisted I bring him in the restaurant. "Not a good idea, Ruth," I cautioned.

"Don't be silly. What possible trouble could he get into?"

Heh, heh. That showed she was from out of town.

I brought Barney in and tied him to the leg of a chair. "Oh, let him loose," said Ruth. "All the food is locked away."

I unbuckled the leash. Barney disappeared on what turned out to be a T-bone tirade. Ten minutes later, as we completed one of the segments, Barney emerged from the kitchen with a $40 chunk of filet in his mouth. Even he seemed surprised at his good fortune.

Ruth's mouth opened wider than Barney's. "How did he do that?"

"I don't know, Ruth. I really don't. But I knew he would."

There must have been a human accomplice, but it remains a mystery.

Ruth took it all very well. But she didn't take my credit card, claiming that Barney was a pretty good testimony to how great her steaks were. "He didn't do this at St. Elmo, did he?" she asked on the air, a little jab at the famous steak restaurant just blocks away.

A year later, a second Indy restaurant in the Ruth's Chris chain had opened. Barney was still in Ruth's good graces despite his previous beef burglary. She was fan of anyone who knew a good cut of meat and that's why she asked her marketing firm in Indy to call me.

"Dick, it's Dan Forst from Caldwell Van Riper. We represent Ruth's Chris Steak House. As you know, we periodically name drinks after celebrities, like Mayor Goldsmith, and radio personality Big John Gillis. Anyway, we have a great idea."

"Dan, why do I think this great idea has nothing to do with naming a drink after Dick Wolfsie?"

"You're right on the money there, Dick. We want to name it after Barney. Isn't that a good idea?"

I couldn't see someone coming into the bar and saying, "Give me a Barney." As with most ideas, it had potential. But Dan and I agreed that it needed a twist. The result was the Barney "Name the Drink" Contest, an opportunity for Channel 8 viewers to create a catchy name that reflected their favorite news hound.

The first problem was getting permission to do this. Paul Karpowicz had recently left the station. The new GM was not opposed to Barney, but being from out of town, he never fully believed in him and his connection to the community.

Promos featuring Barney had dwindled and the new management questioned many of my segments. My new boss felt I was a loose cannon with no one to answer to. He was right about that. I never asked permission for my subject matter. By the time my request would have worked its way up the bureaucratic chain, nothing would have gotten on the air. It is quicker and easier to say you are sorry than to ask permission—that was my time-tested technique and part of my reputation. If I had asked first, I would have never been allowed to have part of my hair transplant live on television, a segment that created quite a buzz (but not a buzz cut) but made the hair on the GM's back stand up. He thought I had traded TV time for the procedure, which was not the case, but I must admit it didn't look good. Although my hair looked great when it was all over.

No, the new guy didn't like the drink contest idea. He thought it would be a mistake to associate Channel 8 news with drinking. The news—everybody's news—was already associated with murder, drug raids, and plane crashes. But "beagles and booze are a bad combo," he said.

I explained to the GM that there were drinks named after Big John Gillis, who did traffic reports, and Mayor Steve Goldsmith, who ran the city. No one had a problem with association. Why did he think this was a mistake? I found out the hard way that the GM felt no overwhelming obligation to explain his reasoning to me.

"We're just not doing it," he said. "Maybe the dog understands English if you don't." Ooo-kay, message received. This was a version of the old "shut up," explained.

I tried one more time, suggesting that we name a nonalcoholic drink after Barney. The answer was still no. See why I hated asking permission?

Then the GM left Channel 8. And just when I was starting to warm up to the guy. Scott Blumenthal, the former sales manager at WISH who had left for a few years to run a sister station, returned to run the station. He, of course, was familiar with Barney's popularity.

I asked for a meeting to discuss this idea with him. It took him only four seconds to say, "Why not?" Barney was going to have a drink named after him. Scott later became one of the station's corporate vice presidents. This may have been his first great decision.

I stuck with the idea of a liquorless drink, surmising that it would lend itself to some funny names, which it did. The contest lasted two weeks. The winner received two free steak dinners and assorted prizes. Here were some of the entries. Take a look. Bottoms up!

K-9 Kooler	Bone Appetite
Barney's Bone Dry	Shot in the Bark
Paws That Refreshes	Pootch Hootch
Barney's 8-Ball	Bare Bones Brew

Hair of the Dog
Virgin Hair
All Bark, No Bite
Tail Chaser
Dog Gone It
Beagle Juice
Designated Woofer
Rabbit Chaser
Hare Raiser

Barney Temple
Biteless Barney
Doggy De Lite
Bone Dry Twist
Barney's Strawberry
Dogaree
Designated Dog
Ears to Ya

So which name do you think won? First, here are the ingredients:

Cranberry juice
Vanilla flavoring
Club soda

Lemon twist

The winner: Barney's All Bark, No Bite
Here's to Barney!

Do You Look Like Barney? How About Your Dog?

Anything that featured Barney started with a leg up, so to speak. Once we organized a morning train ride for the first three hundred viewers who called in to our switchboard. We took the AM die-hards on a short scenic ride through parts of picturesque Indiana, served them breakfast, and returned to the railroad station as the show ended three hours later.

The biggest difficulty on the train was controlling Barney, who now had at his beck and howl three hundred loyal fans who wanted to tell their neighbors they had fed a star. I did anticipate this, so I made an announcement over the train's PA system requesting that "if you must feed him, please just give him a little." Yes, that is what I said. So over the next hour three hundred people gave Barney a piece of their bran muffin and a slice of bacon. Every person on the train felt that Barney was there just to greet him or her. As friendly as I tried to be as I walked the train greeting viewers, it was clear why they had taken the train ride. "Which car is he in now?" people would ask. "Is he coming this way?"

At one point, he lingered at the feet of a woman who was in a wheelchair. He was always drawn to people who were physically challenged. I think he sensed they needed a little extra attention and people in wheelchairs had a much better angle for scratching his ears.

Once he had eaten so much he could barely walk, he crawled up on a seat next to the window to enjoy the scenic view. When the ride finally ended, everyone expressed their gratitude. "Let's do that again soon," many said. No, once was enough, I felt like saying. Based on the way Barney felt when he shuffled off the train, I think he had tired of the high-fiber part of his diet. But he was happy with the bacon.

During the train ride, I chatted with everyone. Opportunities like this provided me with important feedback about what people liked about our morning show. They loved our anchor team and approach to the news, which was much more laid back and informal than the other stations. People also loved to tell me about the dogs in their lives. It did seem that everyone had grown up with a beagle—a beagle, they said, that looked just like Barney.

Bingo. Another idea: A Barney-Look-Alike contest. It was another way to involve viewers in a segment and create a little chatter among people—still the very best way to boost ratings.

Two weeks later, I asked viewers to send me snapshots of their dogs. I would select the top thirty look-alikes and invite the pets and their owners to the studio for the final judging. Beagles are rather distinct, and with the photos I tried to find comparable colorings, weight, and height. I wanted a similar personality to Barney's, too, but that was difficult to discern from a photo.

Somehow I should have okayed this idea with my boss, because the morning of the final beagle-off was total chaos. Thirty howling, sniffing, marking (that's urinating) dogs were in an adjacent news studio. Even during the regular news breaks, viewers at home could hear the beagle convention next door. During the weather portion of the news, I walked on the set and handed meteorologist Randy Olis (who was standing in front of the weather map) six leashes, each connected to a Barney look-alike—and in many cases a Barney act-alike. Randy managed to get through the weather without it affecting his delivery. The rain he predicted for that day, however, never materialized. He later laughed and blamed it on the beagles. Meteorologists at the other stations also got it wrong that day, but they didn't have the fun of being tethered to six hounds.

When the show concluded, I swore I would never do anything quite so hare-brained again. I should have put a Post-It note on my forehead, because three years later it was the *second* Barney Look-Alike Contest.

At the time, I had signed a deal with a local pet store, featuring Barney as its spokesdog. Normally, I resisted mixing my business arrangements with show content, but with this retailer as a sponsor, I could offer some valuable prizes to the winner.

Not only did Pet Supplies Plus offer a $500 shopping spree for the champ, but they also handed out a nifty gift package (dog food, treats, shampoo, leashes) just for showing up at the store. I knew that would bring in the beagle owners and make the contest a success.

I arrived at Pet Supplies Plus at 5 that morning and was elated to see about forty beagles and their masters panting for me. The aroma of the pet store had a stimulating effect on the hounds, who were baying and spraying as only beagles can. The owner went through a lot of paper towels. He was already having an anxiety attack as many of the beagles got off their leashes and were circling the store, sampling different brands of dog treats and taste-testing various brands of food. I realized how similar all beagles were. When hungry—which they always were—they could rip through a bag of dog food in seconds. I admired this because when feeding Barney at home, it usually took me ten minutes to pry open a new pack of Iams.

During each segment of the show, we featured several of the dogs and shared beagle stories on the air. Beagle owners were thrilled that their dogs could meet Barney. Barney was a stray who had become a star. This was America. Live your dream. Anything is possible.

During the show, as I crouched to scratch a few beagle ears, the door of the pet shop opened and in walked a portly gentlemen and his dog—a bulldog. Who, by the way, looked just like his owner. I walked over and bid the man good morning, then broke the news.

"Sir, this is a Barney Look-Alike contest. And that is not a beagle. That is a bulldog."

"Yeah, I know," he grumbled. "So? I'll lose. Now where's my gift package?"

It was another classic Barney moment, not that Barney had delivered the punch line, but that still another viewer had been moved to not just watch the show, but to become part of the legend. This was another story I would repeat dozens of times and it was one of the funniest viewer ad-libs in my television experience. Funnier than most of mine.

Barney, by the way, was not particularly thrilled with the contest idea. Competition for food and attention didn't sit well with him. Oh, he was a good sport about it, but he never warmed up to the winner, Stanley, who was really a younger and more svelte version of Barney. That's show business. Lots of jealousy. And often a pissing contest.

Two look-alike contests were enough, I decided. Enough for both of us.

Barney and
What's-His-Name

Barney changed the way people looked at me. I don't think there was ever any question about this. For my first ten years in Indy, I developed a following. Honestly, the reason people had to follow me was that I kept losing my job and going to another station. In 1982, I lost my initial hosting gig on WISH-TV, then in 1983 my talk show on the independent station WPDS (later Fox) was canceled. I was axed again in 1991 when my morning talk show went off the air. Then in 1994, radio station WIBC lowered the boom.

There are lots of ways to judge success and talent. Lots of ways to spin your situation. Here was mine: I was a survivor; I knew how to reinvent myself; I was multitalented. That all sounded very positive. Or there was this spin: I couldn't keep a job; no one could work with me; the public has spoken. See what I mean?

Yes, I had always bounced back, but my career in Indy had been dangerously on the edge. You don't want your name associated with shows that failed or programs with poor ratings. In addition, I still felt that I was perceived as an outsider.

Hoosiers don't like major changes. Our anchors in Indy had been staples for decades and any changes by management at the top of the newscast were done with great trepidation.

When longtime icons retired, there was a tinge of panic. Who could sit in that anchor chair and make people feel comfortable with the change?

Someone once told me that restaurants in Indiana resisted signs that proclaimed, UNDER NEW MANAGEMENT because Hoosiers preferred the devil they knew to an upstart, even if the food was vile at the old place.

This affinity for "their own" was true across the board. Your pharmacist went to Butler University and your kid's teacher went to Ball State, two central Indiana colleges. Your veterinarian went to Purdue and your ob-gyn attended IU Med School. Then there was Notre Dame. Everyone said he had a brother who went there. You said it even if you were an only child. Indiana was very inbred—not in the same way jokes about Kentucky were intended to suggest, but inbred in the sense of loyalty to their birthplace. Most local celebrities and business successes were home-based. I never saw the stats, but you can't help but feel it. Every time any TV or radio station hired new reporters, they boasted on air that they were Hoosiers, even if they had strayed for a few years and gone out of state. The fact they were returning to their roots went a long way with the public.

As a result, despite my visibility on TV, I felt for a long time like an outsider. Newscasters came to the table with an automatic credibility when they had been born in Indiana. If you hailed from New York, let's say, it became painfully obvious when you had to pronounce cities like Lagoote or Russiaville, which required a deft tongue to say correctly. There was the city of Peru, which was pronounced like the country. But the city of Lebanon was not. The Indiana city of Carmel (pronounced like the candy), I always believed was used as a screening device to weed out those who had tried to slither over the border from Ohio or Illinois. Or came directly from California.

I was from New York. I had a definable attitude and accent. When my wife would listen to one of my interviews on TV, she'd gently suggest that some of my remarks or attempts at humor had a touch of an eastern flavor and might not be appreciated in the Midwest. I resisted that analysis, but I knew in my heart she was right. I once told a long-winded guest to "come back when you have less time." The next day several viewers chided me for the remark. I think in New York I would have been judged with more approbation for the affront.

I was comfortable with my edgy role, and it did make me stand out, but the parade of different jobs may have been a subtle clue that I had not really "made it" in Indiana. The plan had never been to remain in the Midwest. After all, I had been a big star in New York (for six months). I had been sure they'd want me back. Yeah, right.

During the talk show days, it was harder to make conversation with people I'd meet casually. Meteorologists talk about the weather ad nauseam with the public, but it's harder for reporters and talk show hosts because the subject matter they deal with is usually serious and does not lend itself to casual chatter. A friend at another station who covered only crime stories told me that "not too many people just come up and shoot the breeze with me." This, by the way, was quite okay with him. I had many colleagues who preferred a certain anonymity in public. Not me. Not ever.

Once Barney became part of my shtick, the nature of my interaction with the public changed. I was now like the guy (or the gal) in the elevator with a Chihuahua or a Great Dane. Do you want to talk to me? Don't be shy. Just ask about the animal first. Or converse directly with the animal. See how much easier that is?

And what made it even simpler was that he was always with me. Or if he wasn't literally with me (like when I went into a grocery store), he was usually in the car (with the air conditioner or heater on). When I returned from my shopping there would be a crowd of people petting him through the half-open window. As I neared the car, no one ever asked, "Aren't you Dick Wolfsie?" It was always, "Is that Barney?" "It sure is," I would say. Then I'd open the car door and let him come out to greet his fans. I don't think in the hundreds of situations like that I ever answered a single question about me or what I do. The attention was always on Barney.

Funny You Should Ask

What made Barney so funny? I used to have this surreal belief that he had a sense of humor. Let's get serious.

Here's the truth. Dogs are, well, dogs. They enter our human world and we expect them to act like dogs. Right? Not really. In fact, most of us have a set idea of how our canines should behave. Tail wagging is cool. So is sitting and rolling over on command. But that's a short list. We keep dogs on a short leash, so to speak.

I'm always amused when I a hear a dog owner reeling off a list of his or her pet's virtues: He doesn't mess in the house, she doesn't climb on the furniture, he doesn't chew things, she doesn't leave the food all around her bowl, he doesn't bark at other dogs, she doesn't pull me when we go for a walk, he doesn't run away, etc., etc. Notice anything about this list? It's all negatives, all things the poor dog doesn't do! Well, not having a dog achieves pretty much the same results, at considerably less cost in money and effort. The point is, these behaviors are natural. When someone says about your dog,

161

"Oh, he's such a good boy," what they mean is: you've managed to suck the real dog out of him.

Now, in all fairness, I have heard dog owners boast about their pets' naughtiness or how spoiled they are. But usually these are endearing behaviors . . . and tolerable. Like when your toddler smears cake all over his face at his birthday party.

The cool part about being a dog owner is that you have power. You are a control freak. I know you don't want to hear this, but it's true. There's this dog whisperer on TV who says he hates long leashes because it lets the dog think he's the boss. Barney was always on a long leash. I paid the price and reaped the rewards.

What made Barney a hoot is that I let him be a dog in a human world. He was sometimes naughty, sometimes nice, and occasionally nuts. Not just in the regular human world, but in the manufactured, often rehearsed world of TV. If your dog ate four sticks of butter (like Barney once did) you'd be ticked: at the expense, the mess, the diarrhea. Basically I let Barney be himself. I let him go where his instincts led him. Do not try this at home with a teenager. Everything I ever aspired to on TV, Barney achieved through the niche that his very nature afforded him. I wanted to be unpredictable. I wanted people to wonder, "Gee, what will Dick do today?" I had to work hard at that, but not the dog. For him it was natural. Dogs don't have day planners.

And yet, I did wonder sometimes. Did he have a sense of humor? A natural sense of timing? His unpredictability was damn predictable in the sense that you knew he was going to do something funny. Case in point: Damien Mason was a very talented Bill Clinton impersonator who came on the show during the 2000 presidential campaign.

I rarely did in-studio interviews, but the satellite truck was broken and this kind of exchange really did work better in a seated arrangement. In cases like this, Barney occupied the third seat on the set, happy to chill out and snooze during the chat.

I was seated to Mason's right, Barney to his left. But this time Barney sat straight up in his seat for the duration of the exchange. As Mason delivered one-liners lampooning the president, Barney was attentive. As the interview wrapped in the third and final segment, Mason turned to Barney and asked: "Barney, I'm not happy with Al Gore. How about being on the ticket with me as vice president?"

Barney turned, looked at the comic, shook his head abruptly, jumped off the chair, and disappeared as the cameras followed him out the studio door. Anchor Dave Barras made the oddest remark. "I swear, that was totally unrehearsed," he said, as viewers heard the camera crew burst into laughter. Did he think that the dog had writers? Could he read a teleprompter?

Barney took one famous bit after another right out of a playbook. One spring we arranged a visit to observe the Carmel High School baseball team in practice. Five AM was not their normal start time for a workout, but the coach wanted a little publicity for the team, which was on a winning tear and had one of the best pitchers in the state.

I interviewed the coach in the first segment and then as the sun came up we decided to show the celebrated hurler in action. The first athlete struck out on three blinding fastballs. Barney was sitting on the bench enjoying the attention of the rest of the team. At the plate, the next batter swung wildly, squiggling a ball down the left infield foul line. Barney scampered off the bench, grabbed the ball while it was still rolling, and headed for the outfield.

Dick Wolfsie

"Hey!" screamed the coach. "That's our only ball!" With that, all the players ditched their gloves and pursued Barney. The bench emptied as well, reminiscent of the onset of a brawl in professional sports.

I stood there with the same thought I always had. If I had arranged this, planned it, rehearsed it, it would have never happened. If this were a movie scene with a "professional" dog, who knows how many takes it would have required.

Here's another Barney moment I didn't rehearse. And couldn't have. During an early morning segment to promote the opening of a new restaurant, the musicians hired to play some authentic Mexican music lacked a certain something: talent. The first two segments bordered on something you wouldn't want to hear on the border. In segment three, their electric banjos mercilessly ceased to function. This was not an act of selflessness; it was the result of Barney's removing the extension cord from the wall with his teeth and then enjoying his high-fiber (wire?) snack. Everyone's a critic.

Even the harshest entertainment critic would have given Barney an A for perfect comedic timing in this one. At the opening of the new Westin Hotel in downtown Indy, I did the show from their lobby—in my pajamas, pretending I was a guest of the hotel. The Westin was promoting one of its highly touted new, state of the art mattresses. The manager suggested I order breakfast and have it delivered to my "room." I ordered two pieces of bacon, not good for anything coronary, but great for the comedy. I figured Barney would jump on the bed and devour both pieces in one huge bite while I pretended to be too engaged with my guest to notice. That's not how Barney saw it. He hopped up and took one piece. Then he leaped off the bed, waited a few comic beats while he gobbled his treat, then returned again, each trip stealing a single slice. But he didn't

164

snatch it; he slowly and meticulously slid it off the plate by placing the end in his mouth and backing away. Why get just one big laugh when you can milk the premise for a few minutes?

The bottom line was that there existed this palpable anticipation by every viewer that at some point between 5 AM and 7 AM every weekday there was an awfully good chance that Barney was going to be a dog. Not a well-behaved canine from a nice family with good breeding, but a real dog. And real trouble. And real funny.

Viewers were charmed by his natural dogginess. They didn't worry about his discipline or feel responsibility for his unsocial behavior. Everyone was like Barney's grandparent, especially me.

At the same time, I had to be a real parent, and I remained aware that Brett's perception of my relationship with the dog posed potential problems. Calling it jealousy might be an oversimplification, but when I was out with Brett and Barney, people would come up to me and say, "Wow, that's the dog from TV." It was rare in the beginning for anyone to address Brett. I learned to minimize the effect of this by always first saying to fans, "Hi folks, say hello to my son, Brett." That gave Brett the chance to play his role as the beleaguered brother and say, "And that's Barney. Be sure you don't have anything edible in your pockets. He's real trouble around food." Even with this, Brett avoided opportunities for the three of us to go out together. He felt invisible. And it broke my heart. It did motivate me to do even more things with him without the dog. In an odd way, it might have even brought Brett and me closer.

Fair Game

Both Barney and Brett loved the Indiana State Fair. There were always so many WISH-TV fans in the crowd that it was hard to get from one end of the grounds to the other without stopping dozens of times to talk to people and let them meet the real star. In all the years Barney and I appeared on TV, I never brought my son to the fair with Barney, and vice versa. I was smart enough to know that father-and-son time didn't require a mascot.

Before I came to the Midwest, I had never been to a State Fair. I'm from New York City. I didn't even know that New York had a fair. People tell me it's upstate, wherever that is. I didn't know what I was missing.

The Indiana State Fairgrounds occupies 250 sprawling acres at the major intersection of 38th Street and Fall Creek Parkway, just a few minutes northeast of the statehouse and WISH-TV. The event is over 150 years old and has been at this location since 1892.

While the fairgrounds hosts hundreds of events throughout the year, people venture from every corner of Indiana in August for the State Fair. These folks parade their livestock, enter their pies in contests, take part in sheep-shearing competitions, and sell their arts and crafts. And, yes, stuff their faces.

For many, a day at the fair is just an excuse to graze the main drag, sipping on icy Lemon Shake-Ups and gnawing on huge turkey legs or pork chops the size of a small laptop. Sugar-dusted elephant ears, crispy onion rings, roasted ears of corn, and the time-honored grilled cheese sandwiches are all favorites. Even health-conscious Hoosiers anticipate their annual trek to indulge in an Italian sausage on a bun with sautéed onions and green peppers, along with an overflowing plate of greasy curly fries. How about a deep-fried Oreo cookie for dessert? Hey, it's just once a year.

There's so much to see: Brett loved the state marching band championships and the pageant that selects the Fair Queen. Mary Ellen has a thing for the baby rabbits and exotic chickens. I look forward to the demolition derby and—I hate to admit this—baton twirling. There is clogging. I hate clogging. Then I see it at the fair. And I still hate it.

For the almost 800,000 people each year who spend a day at the fair, this is more than a trip, it is a tradition. Grandparents love to share memories with their grandkids. But they won't share their deep-fried sauerkraut balls. Get your own.

There is a distinctive odor to the Indiana State Fair, but only the uninitiated, the newcomers, are put off by it. For all others, it is a rite of nasal passage, and a reminder to Hoosiers that the long days of summer are almost over.

The fair was an easy week for me in the sense that there were always new acts and exhibits to cover. The bad news was every station in town—and many from outside central Indiana—also covered the event, so the chances of airing something exclusive were rare. One year, every station featured the pig races, where the oinkers lumbered around a track at some surprising speeds to get back to their cozy pens. Only WISH-TV added a dog in the competition. Watching Barney race four pigs was must-see TV. He lost, by the way. I don't think he realized they were potential pork chops.

No one liked the annual Indiana State Fair more than Barney. We went to twelve of them. All those years of corn dogs and deep-fried Twinkies kinda blend together in my mind—what's left of it. Barney loved the fair for the exact same reason that all Hoosiers did: he loved cholesterol-laden food, animal smells, and country music concerts. Okay, maybe not the third one. Although we did sit through a George Strait concert once and he only howled twice. The dog, I mean.

Each August when we drove through the gate, every parking lot attendant took the time to come over and stroke Barney, his head sticking out the window, his nose twitching at record speed. Occasionally, an employee who was not familiar with Barney questioned whether you could bring a pet to the fair, which always made me laugh because there were thousands of pigs, cows, and chickens just a sniff away.

Once Barney realized where he was, he'd go into a frenzy, fully aware that there was a cornucopia of smells awaiting him. After a segment from the fair demonstrating the proper way to make a deep-fried pickle, for example, we would walk down the main drag, greeting people. If I saw in my radar any small children with food walking toward us, I always called ahead and issued a warning: *Please ask your children to guard their food. If there is food in your baby carriage, please secure it.*

This never worked and on more than one occasion, as Barney and I were hustling down the main drag, Barney extricated a hot dog or a burrito right from a youngster's grip as we sped by. Sometimes it scared the kids, but most of the victims' parents were fans of the show and felt honored to have been an official casualty of his stealth. Yes, they would brag about this. Now they had a personal Barney story to share with their friends and neighbors.

During a typical fair, patrons saw Barney ride on the Ferris wheel, enter the pig race, cavort with rabbits (they made him nervous; so much for breeding), and get kicked by a horse. He rode in mini-race cars, sat on tractors, and took a bite out of a huge statue of a chicken carved out of butter. He did almost everything a regular fairgoer did, except pay to get in. Incredibly, he seemed to remember places he had been to the previous year, and made it clear which venues he wanted to return to.

Each year, our first appearance at the fair was the morning of the annual balloon race. Thousands of people lined the infield of the horse track waiting for thirty balloons to lift gracefully into the sky around 6 AM Barney and I reported from the balloon race for twelve years. Much of the crowd was composed of WISH-TV fans, born and bred Hoosiers who made it a tradition to attend the first day of the fair.

Most of the balloons were huge floating advertisements for everything from real estate companies to local wineries. If you were a big Jack Daniel's fan, you could stumble out of bed and watch a 2,500-square-foot bottle of whiskey float across the sky. How about a huge Burger King Whopper? The sky was the limit.

Part of the balloon race ritual was my annual interview with various city and state dignitaries. Frank O'Bannon, then lieutenant governor, was always there because he was also the unofficial head of the Department of Agriculture, so any time he could get on TV and somehow work the word "corn" into a sentence, it made political hay—another word he got in a lot. Somehow he also managed to sneak in a few references to beef, pork, and poultry. The guy was good. Ditto regarding his wife, Judy, a class act who just loved Barney and would come over every year during the balloon race just to give him a hug. Every year, I could read the lieutenant governor's lips prior to the interview as he asked his aide what my name was. Remembering Barney's name was never a problem for him.

When the governor, Evan Bayh, went on to become a U.S. senator, O'Bannon was elected to the top state office, but he never abandoned his obligation to the fair and always stopped by to see Barney and me. It would be years later that both Barney and this beloved Indiana politician would make their final visit to the fair the very same summer.

There was another tradition that I upheld. I would interview a balloon pilot, he would tell me how safe ballooning was, then he would ask me to go up with him, and then I would chicken out. I was not afraid of flying; I was afraid of crashing. The truth is, the sport is quite safe, so I often used Barney as an excuse, claiming he was afraid of heights.

One Balloon Day morning just prior to leaving the house, I peeked out my window and immediately called the station. The clouds were thick, dark, and menacing, but rain had not yet fallen. Randy, our weatherman, told me that there was a chance of heavy precipitation and possibly lightning, both of which would effectively cancel the annual festivities. As far as I knew, this had never happened before, but Barney and I headed out the door as usual for our first segment, scheduled for 5:15 AM Even if the race was going to be called off, I still needed to fill my three spots in the morning news.

These kinds of last-minute changes were a challenge, so they really got the adrenaline going. How do you do a segment about a balloon race when there are no balloons, there are no balloonists, and there are no bystanders? That was the prospect I faced if the prediction for heavy rain became a reality.

Once we arrived at the fairgrounds, we headed under the tunnel to the infield, an area surrounded by a horse track where every morning the trotters and pacers would get their early morning workout. As I drove onto the field behind the station van, you could see that people had already gathered for the balloon event. For many families this was the beginning of a tradition because the balloon race was only a few years old. But the idea of starting a ritual that could last generations had great appeal to Hoosiers. The fair always has been about custom and history.

The chants for Barney started as soon he stuck his head out of the car window. Once I parked, a line formed. I began signing pictures of Barney, sketching in his paw print with a black Magic Marker.

The downpour began about 5:30. Barney and I rushed back to seek shelter with my photographer, who had opted not to put up the mast atop the satellite truck, the device that sends the live signal back to the station. Putting an antenna up in a thunderstorm was just asking for trouble—like holding up your two-iron on the golf course—so we decided to sit tight and see if the skies would clear.

I took a call from the producer back at the station and was temporarily distracted. When I turned around, Barney was gone. Most dogs do not like rain. Barney included. But this was the State Fair and already the meaty aroma from the vendors had wafted toward the infield. He was off. And I couldn't search for him. I was scheduled to be on in ten minutes.

I looked out on the infield and saw a rotund man standing in a huge puddle of water. Did I say rotund? Let me revise. His potbelly protruded out almost a foot from his belt. He must have weighed 500 pounds. Water cascaded down around his mammoth physique. Apparently, he was in charge of the final decision as to the running of the balloon race. It looked like he had a tri-corder from the old *Star Trek* series. It was some kind of device that gave him immediate contact with the National Weather Service.

And Barney? His wanderlust had become a touch water-logged, so he had situated himself between this man's legs, under his belly, using the man's girth as protection from the elements.

Every time the man moved, Barney repositioned himself. It was like a well choreographed dance. If the man moved forward, Barney moved with him. If he stepped back, Barney retreated. Even this guy was getting a kick out of Barney's well-timed avoidance of the rain.

Unfortunately, this was never seen on TV. Remember, we hadn't been on the air, but hundreds of rabid balloon fans who had not left the fairgrounds did see this classic moment.

Portrait of the Artist as a Young Pup

Barney never attained the kind of stature enjoyed by Elvis Presley, but a few comparisons should not go unnoticed. Both celebrities enjoyed doughnuts and peanut butter, and both were favorite subjects of artists who captured the charm and charisma of these unique personalities through every imaginable medium. Happily, there is no known depiction of Barney on a velvet canvas. I happily yield that distinction to the King.

Over the years, packages arrived via UPS, bundles appeared on my desk at the TV station, and boxes were just dumped on my front porch. The contents were the true spectrum of trash to treasure, but every painting, carving, sculpture, or drawing represented a genuine attempt by viewers—whether they had a smidgen of talent or not—to feel a part of Barney's legacy. Now their love of this little street dog had been expressed in a very concrete way. And one time it actually was concrete. This was their method of saying thanks for all the smiles and laughs Barney provided every morning.

It reached the point where "Barney" was all over the house. He was on the walls, in drawers, under our bed, on shelves in the garage, on the pool table in the basement. Unlike promotional T-shirts that I was given after a TV remote, I couldn't possibly discard or give away any of this memorabilia that slowly but surely was taking over my house like the plant in *Little Shop of Horrors*. On rare occasions when I was on a cleaning binge, I would chuck something, then hours later I'd fish it out of the garbage, wondering how the elderly woman from Tipton would feel if she knew I was trashing her pen and ink drawing of her favorite TV celebrity.

Mary Ellen agreed that we couldn't discard anything, but she didn't want the living room to look like the pub at the North American Hunting Club, so only two pieces of art found a place in the living room. Translation: my wife picked what she liked best and proclaimed: "And this shall represent all the other stuff in the house that shall not be in plain sight." Not many things get to be in our living room without going through a strict Mary Ellen selection and screening process. For example, I have an Emmy Award. Would you like to see it? I'll meet you in my basement.

One piece she loved was the work of Bill Arnold. He was not a painter, or a musician, and not a photographer. He was a . . . I have no idea what you would call him. He made things out of barbed wire. That's right, barbed wire. With nothing but a small, specially made pair of pliers and hundreds of feet of wire (usually one long piece) he could twist the material into virtually anything. No blueprints, no plans; just a vision in his head. He mostly made animals—birds, foxes, beavers, bears, horses. Each one was life-size. I think Bill was a genius, but a lousy businessman. One day he just left town. Gone but not forgotten. His life-size deer sits in front of the entrance to the Indianapolis Zoo, as do several other pieces of his artwork throughout the park.

How good was he? He once crafted a bald eagle and secured it on top of a telephone pole on I-70. It drove the folks at the Department of Natural Resources crazy because they got dozens of calls about the poor, sick (and endangered) national symbol that clearly required some medical attention—it hadn't moved in days. Motorists pulled off the side of the road and clapped their hands in an attempt to rouse the bird. When the DNR made Bill take it down, he put the eagle in a cage on his front lawn. Then the Humane Society started getting calls. That's how good he was.

I invited Bill on the show and asked him to give a demonstration of his artwork. I called him the day before the scheduled remote.

"Bill, it's Dick Wolfsie. Just wanted to know if you had any idea of what you wanted to make on the show."

"Well, Dick, would you like me to make a statue of Barney?"

"Gee, Bill, that never crossed my mind. That's a great idea." It was always better when the guest thought it was his brainstorm.

We did the show and explained the process he had perfected. The total project to make Barney would take about twelve hours and almost 300 feet of wire. We couldn't broadcast every twist and turn, so we had to do another show to unveil the final product. A few days later, Bill revealed a masterpiece in wire, so realistic in its own way that it even captured Barney's personality. Yes, there was even a touch of mischief in his barbed-wire posture. So, I'd put the wire sculpture as my number-one favorite.

The second piece is a glorious pencil drawing of Barney by Debra DeFazio based on the photo taken by Ed Bowers several years earlier. So many paintings and drawings of Barney over the years, but none captured his personality more than this one. Those eyes. Man, did she capture his eyes.

There is a close third—not good enough to pass Mary Ellen's muster for a place in the living room, but close just the same.

That piece of art comes from Rob Taylor, founder of Forth Dimension Holographics, in Nashville, Indiana. Entering his shop, you enter, well, another dimension. It is one of the few places in America where you can have a hologram made of yourself or your children. Hey, how about your pet? Holograms are realistic and very creepy. It's like the subject is actually inside the frame suspended in some kind of animation.

The original photo, taken in 1997 as part of a segment on *Daybreak,* is a dual hologram. Look at it from one angle and there I am; take a glance from the other side and you see Barney. According to Rob, when this piece was hanging in his shop, Barney received far more second looks than I did. "He holographed better," said Rob.

A copy of the hologram hangs above my desk in my home office. It does require some special lighting to make it come alive, but it still gives me goose bumps when I see Barney staring back at me. If you are ever in Nashville, Indiana, you can see it, too.

So those are my favorites. But everything else is a three-way tie: the beagle walking stick, the watercolor painting, the carved beagle tree stump; the embroidered beagle pillow; the beagle clock; the chalk drawings; the ice sculpture; the wax candle, the neon sign. The list is endless. I have never thrown anything away. Although the ice sculpture did melt.

Puppy Love

As Barney became more and more of an intergenerational hit, he and I visited scores of elementary schools. Any dog is a hit at a school, but our walks up and down the corridors created quite a commotion. My speech was brief to the kids, usually just an opportunity to tell the kids to encourage their parents to watch the show along with some safety tips about petting dogs. I threw in a little beagle history, too, just to make the presentation a touch more educational.

My favorite response to a question was from a third-grader. I was explaining how a beagle's hearing and sense of smell are excellent, but the eyesight was not quite as good. I phrased the question a bit inelegantly, I guess. "What sense is Barney lacking in?" I asked.

"Common sense," said a kid who never missed the show.

Inevitably, the teacher would follow up our visit with an assignment to the class to write a thank-you note to Dick and Barney.

For a long time, I just let the stack pile up, assuming that each letter was simply the perfunctory thank-you and a sophomoric drawing of Barney. I kept these in a huge box over the years and, quite honestly, had not read many of them. Then one day in one of those mad housecleaning moments, I decided that if I was going to discard them, in good conscience, I had a responsibility to read them—every single one.

Here are some of my favorites, slightly edited. I only picked the ones that made me laugh out loud.

Dear Mr. Wolfsie,

Thanks for coming to our school. I would like to watch you and Barney on TV, but my mom just lets us watch stuff that is educational.

***

Dear Mr. Wolfsie,

I love your dog. I think he is smarter than my brother. Is he for sale?

Ernie

***

Dear Dick and Barney,

Thanks for coming to our school. Can you come for dinner some night? My mom would love that. I'm not sure about my dad.

Love,
Kaitlyn

***

Dear Dick and Barney,

Thanks for coming to visit us. We were all very happy. Mainly because Mrs. Potter canceled the test.

Lana

***

Dear Mr. Wolfsie,

It was very cool when Barney crawled on his belly when he wanted something. My father can do that.

Eric

***

Dear Dick and Barney,

My teacher said any of us could grow up to be like you, but just in case we don't, we should study hard.

Love, Toni

***

Dear Mr. Wolfsie,

Who makes more money, you or Barney? I have watched you on TV and you should split it.

Effie

***

Dear Barney,

Thanks for coming to our school. And for bringing Dave with you.

Love,
Erika

***

Dear Dick and Barney,

My dad said that you needed a dog to get people to like you. I really don't like dogs. Will a cat work?

Jona

***

Dear Mr. Wolfsie,

Where do you work? I see you on TV in the morning sometimes. But where do you work?

Anna

Yes, it was hard to think of what I did as work. With all the pressures and politics of TV, I had a job that wasn't really a job. I wore jeans; I brought my dog; I met new and interesting people every day. I didn't go to a factory every morning, I went to a Frisbee contest; I didn't work at a bank, I went to a banjo convention. I didn't have to show up at the office. I just had to show off.

Touched by a Beagle

Barney seemed to grow more comfortable in his skin as the years passed.

"A major part of his success was that he was so comfortable with people," Lee Giles recalls. "He never lost his patience, especially with the kids."

But it wasn't just little people. Barney and I first met Sandy Allen at a charity event in the early nineties. She was the tallest woman in the world. All seven feet seven inches of her loved Barney. On several occasions we also visited her in the retirement village where she lived. Sandy had a rough life. She was born in Chicago, then left by her mother and raised by her grandmother. She once observed that she was kind of like Barney—abandoned at birth, never fully appreciated. Barney always jumped onto a chair so Sandy could pet him. Kneeling or reaching down to the floor was virtually impossible due to her size.

Sandy's height was both a liability and an advantage. To be sure, her abnormal tallness afforded her some opportunities in life, but this required calling attention to her stature, like when she was hired as a greeter at the Ripley's Believe It or Not Museum in Canada. Her whole life she had to endure both the ridicule of others and the sheer complexities of getting through a day dealing with problems posed by her size—like finding a pair of size 17 shoes. She used humor, just like Barney and me. When people would ask, "What do you eat?" she'd point to her T-shirt, emblazoned with the phrase, "I love short people. I had three for lunch."

When Sandy had a bout with some health issues, Barney would jump up on her specially made bed (no small leap) and nuzzle himself against her. Sandy would beam and remark, "Thanks for bringing Barney; he's the only reason I watch the show." Then she'd ask if that hurt my feelings. It didn't. I was used to it.

Accepting others regardless of their looks, size, or mental ability was Sandy's mission in life. It was also Barney's. Happily, dogs don't make such distinctions, but Barney's public display of total acceptance probably served as a lesson to all who watched. The message was: we all should be more like Barney—more loving, more tolerant.

Sandy died in August 2008. She had remained upbeat until the end but had clearly tired of her battle against the restrictions placed on her by her own body. The local stations ran video of the assisted-living home in Shelbyville, Indiana, where Sandy resided. In a shot of her room, a photo of Barney was clearly evident on the bulletin board above her bed. They were together at the end. She was truly his biggest fan.

As a television reporter, I was attracted to stories like Sandy's, tales of people who dealt with prejudice and discrimination.

But remote live TV did not always lend itself to issues as heavy as this. A taped package or a longer format program give you more time and the luxury to develop the subject.

But during my morning spots I had only three minutes each hour—barely enough time to ask a couple of basic questions.

That's why I was torn when a local support group of parents whose children had Down syndrome contacted me about doing a program highlighting their efforts.

How could I raise awareness of the organization, spread the word that support was available for new parents, and do it responsibly in three-minute intervals? Oh, and still make the show light and entertaining? Remember, I was supposed to provide the break from hard news.

After exchanging a number of phone calls with the executive director of the support group, I began searching for an angle. I needed more than talking heads, an insider reference to shows where nothing is happening, just people yakking at the host.

I was good at finding a hook to hang a show on. Potential guests were not. They knew that they wanted to get on TV but didn't grasp the visual nature of the medium. "Can't we just talk about our event?" they would ask. The answer was no. I needed more than that.

"Do all the youngsters ever get together?" I asked the president of the Down Syndrome Support group, still in search of a show concept. "Well, next week, we're making a calendar to raise money and we have to meet with the photographer and all the families."

Whoa! There it was. Problem solved. We'd do a photo shoot with these adorable children. We'd observe the artistic process as it unfolded with the subjects and the photographer.

Barney and I arrived at 4:45 AM I don't think the photographer had ever been up that early in her life, but she knew what a superb opportunity this was to publicize a unique group of children, as well as her craft.

We did the first segment with the photographer, talking about the challenge she faced in creating a dozen different shots that would send a positive message about these kids. When the children arrived a little later, they were antsy. I looked at the photographer's face. She knew this was going to be a very, very long morning and she had to "perform" on live TV.

At one point, the photographer wanted all ten children in one shot, preferably sitting on the daybed in her studio. The parents put their toddlers in place, but this was kind of like herding cats, as each child tried to scramble away, often grasping and crying for Mom and Dad. The chaos added to the youngsters' anxieties and I could see some genuine fear in their precious faces. I worried about the idea of using the kids for pure entertainment purposes. I certainly didn't want anyone to think I was exploiting the children.

Enter Barney. He had been sitting next to me, watching the chaotic activity. Suddenly he sprang onto the bed and situated himself between this mass of humanity that was spread out across the mattress. The kids squealed and began, well, pawing at Barney. The wrapped their arms around him and lavished him with kisses. In their exuberance, several children literally fell on top of him as they jockeyed for position to pet him. He never batted an adorable brown eye. Instead, he just basked in their attention, attention that almost bordered on abuse. It mattered not. This was classic Barney. Somehow, some way, he knew these kids required a different posture on his part. And later when I saw the photos that were snapped at that instant, it confirmed what an extraordinary moment it was.

Just as extraordinary was the morning Barney and I spent with Emily Hunt, one of the bravest little girls I have ever met. She had been thrown from a ride at an amusement park in northern Indiana and was paralyzed from the waist down. In addition, the accident had killed Emily's fifty-seven-year-old grandmother. A fun family outing had turned tragic for the Hunt family. The case had a devastating effect on the family but resulted in her dad's commitment to not only Emily's future but the plight of all those suffering from spinal cord injuries.

Emily attends school on a regular basis. She still holds on to her dream of one day becoming a professional dancer. Her courageous spirit and determination have been an inspiration to many in Indianapolis, the state, and the nation.

I wanted to help publicize the foundation that her father, Mike, had set up to fund research in this kind of paralysis. Doing the show required that Mike, like all guests, rise bright and early to appear on camera. He was pessimistic about Emily's participation because at that time (she was only six) bathing and dressing, as well as connecting the necessary breathing apparatus, was time consuming and would have meant getting her up literally in the middle of the night.

Emily was not a morning person, I was warned, but I knew that her presence on the show would impact the viewers emotionally and that this would lead to increased attendance at the annual fund-raising walk around the Indianapolis Motor Speedway.

To make it easier on Emily, Mike allowed us to bring the camera into her room and talk to her while she was still in bed. The bed was very high off the ground, a necessary adjustment so that caregivers could more easily dress her and pick her up to move her to the wheelchair.

I walked into the room, Barney trailing behind me. Emily produced the expected scowl. I felt horribly guilty about the intrusion, although my motives were pure, as Mike knew. What could I do to cheer her up? What, indeed? Barney took a flying leap onto the bed, possibly a record for a vertical jump by a beagle, beating the record set with Sandy Allen's bed by a hair. He rolled over on his back, incredibly positioning himself right alongside Emily. Sadly, she could not scratch him, but her smile lit up the room.

Any dog could boost a little girl's spirit, but this was different. Barney was not his usual hyperactive self. He had responded to her situation by kicking it down a notch. It seemed they just looked into each other's eyes for the longest time. How much of this was in my imagination, I don't know, but I can't recall another situation that touched me more.

Maybe your dog would have done that very same thing. But Barney did it in front of 100,000 people, no doubt pumping up the fund-raising for Mike Hunt's foundation for people with spinal cord injuries.

I felt very good about my job that day. Any time I had the opportunity to use my unique role to help others was a plus. Sure, I had a huge ego; I loved the attention and the notoriety, but it was also important to me that I not squander that time each morning. Few people in my business had the freedom to say and do anything they wanted for ten minutes every morning in front of tens of thousands of people. Sometimes the segment was a riot. But it was always a responsibility—to either entertain or to educate. Or the perfect form: do both at once.

Mike Hunt sent me a photo a few weeks later that he had taken during the show. And this is one of the photos I treasure most. This is what Barney was all about. Take a look at it. And then you'll understand, as I did, Barney's mission in life.

By the way, Mike and Emily wrote a book called *Emily's Walk,* the story of how one courageous little girl faced incredible challenges early in her life. Book signings always were a success, but the day that she and Barney teamed up together broke all sales records. That was a combo that was hard to beat.

Travels with Barney

Barney was always next to me, eyes on me like a laser. During book signings at malls, he loved the attention from fans but even a short trip to the men's room resulted in a touch of separation anxiety (for both of us).

He was visibly agitated when I was not in plain sight, straining his neck to see where I went. I usually offered a free book to a customer if he or she would watch Barney while I went to the bathroom. But this had some serious drawbacks. On several occasions he got off the leash he was tethered to and scampered down the mall, his legs in a whirl as he tried to negotiate the slippery vinyl floor at each turn.

"He went that-a-way," my supposed dog watcher would say as I returned to my table. I would bolt down the mall, occasionally catching sight of him, but he would disappear around a corner. No problem: I just had to look for him in 200 stores. I needed an excuse to go into Victoria's Secret anyway.

I'd walk into each shop and ask the clerk if he had seen a male, tri-colored beagle. I realized how stupid it was to offer a description. There were not a great many stray dogs in the mall on any given day. Eventually I would find him. He was never surprised to see me. Remember, that was part of the game.

Because Barney was so unhappy alone I seldom left home without him, making us potential stars for the next American Express commercial.

Mary Ellen had encouraged—no, demanded—my constant stewardship of Barney over the years because of his destructive nature. "If you go, he goes." This had a much less ominous sound than her dictum years earlier, "If he stays, I go." We had made some progress.

When my second book, *Dick Wolfsie's New Book: Longer, Funnier, Cheaper,* was published, the concept was that people would come into the bookstore and say, "Do you have Dick Wolfsie's *New Book?*" That was funny until my third book came out. Now the title made no sense at all and just confused the buyers and the sellers. Other than all that, it was a great idea.

Barney's picture was on both covers—mine, too, but Barney had been absolutely no help with those books. That was the extent of Barney's involvement in the whole process . . . just waiting for a walk and dinner while I sat all day at the computer trying to think of witty things. They were just Andy Rooney/Dave Barry kinds of musings about everyday life. It was easy. If something funny occurred to me, I wrote it down. But as Mark Twain said, "It's not the writing that's hard, it's the occurring."

It was time for something different. When a Connecticut publisher was looking for authors around the country to compile books of roadside oddities and unique people in each of the fifty states, she contacted me about Indiana. Sadly, she did not have the strength to give Barney a good belly rub, but her smile lit up the room, enough of a treat for both of us.

I was flattered by her interest, but I was leaning against accepting the offer for the following reason: It was a whole lot of work. It meant traveling to all ninety-two counties to search for these oddities. I did know central Indiana, but that was only 20 percent of the state. I hadn't the slightest idea about the other seventy or so counties. It was another world. Much of it was more rural, for one, and there were over 2,000 cities on the map, many with just a few hundred people.

Where would I begin? There was no way I could do this.

But I knew I couldn't use lack of time as an excuse because I had an incredibly flexible schedule. I was on TV for two hours each weekday morning, but booking the segments and pre-interviewing guests could be spread out over a week or done in one full marathon afternoon. No, I needed a better pretext to avoid this new challenge.

How about this: I cannot follow directions, a talent I assumed was a prerequisite to traveling the state in search of material for the book. Compass and map—I can make a very funny limerick using those two words, but I couldn't find my way out of a Plymouth minivan. On a map, north is up, south is down. I can't make this concept work for me in a three-dimensional world. I might have been the right person to write this travelogue but I was the worst one to go out and research it. That's what I was going to tell the editor when she called back for my decision.

My wife had a different view. Mary Ellen felt that if I declined this offer and someone else wrote the book, it would haunt me that I had turned it down. "You'll do nothing but whine about what a poor job this person did. You'll complain he can't write, that he wasn't funny and how he missed all the good stuff." Boy, she nailed it. That's exactly the kind of annoying thing I was apt to do.

As for my concern about directions, Mary Ellen made a good point. "Dick, so what if you get lost? You don't know where you're going anyway, so get in the car and drive. That's how you'll find neat stuff. Oh, and take the dog with you."

That part appealed to me. It reminded me of the book *Travels with Charley,* John Steinbeck's chronicle of his cross-country journey with his French poodle, Charley.

There was clearly an effort here to get us out of the house on weekends, but Mary Ellen's logic was impeccable. Before I made my final decision, I looked at the copy of *Texas Curiosities* that the editor had originally sent me. I decided to thumb through the book and stop at a random page. If what I read on that page reflected the kind of wacky stuff I wanted to write about, that would seal the deal. Whenever I was on the fence about something I always looked for some kind of sign for the right thing to do. I even did it for this book, as you'll see later.

I flipped to page 78 and there it was: A story about a Jernigan's Taxidermy shop in Waco, Texas. Jeremy Jernigan specializes in stuffing the rear ends of the animals. His store window apparently is filled with animal butts. Even Barney could have found this curiosity. With his nose in the air. Enough read. I decided to do it.

Sadly, there was no taxidermist of that sort in Indiana, so while I never found someone who did that kind of stuffing, I did find some neat stuff. For over a year, Barney and I traveled Indiana—six thousand miles, more than three hundred cities (visiting two thousand was just not possible). Virtually every weekend we'd head out either Friday afternoon or

Saturday morning and spend the entire day (and often overnight) nosing our way around small towns, pumping locals for
information about their area to find an anomaly that would
lend itself to a chapter in the book.

I talked with local news editors and county historians
hoping they would point me in the right direction. I always
hoped they literally pointed, because north, south, east, and
west were a mystery to me.

The historians were fixated on what had happened
hundreds of years ago, but no one wants to pack the three
kids in the Ford pickup to visit a historical marker in the
middle of nowhere or in the middle of downtown, for that
matter. I think it's cool that James Buchanan once fell off
his horse on this street in downtown New Palestine, but it's
not something you'd want to visit. Or maybe it was Millard
Fillmore. See, who cares?

The visitor and convention bureaus were of little help
because their inclination was to push places that they were
promoting on their own Web sites and through brochures.
Repeating what was already in the PR pipeline was a big
waste of time and not what the publisher was looking for.

Newspaper editors were sometimes grumpy and often
too busy, which meant they were damn good editors, just no
help to me. Incredibly, even men and women who had lived
and worked in these tiny towns their whole lives were at a
loss to come up with something offbeat in the area. When
I ventured to these towns, I'd inquire about local oddities at
a gas station, a café, or a barbershop. I often got this kind of
response: "Nothing special here, young man. Lived here all
my life. Can't think of a thing."

I kept asking the question, mostly because I liked being
called "young man." Truth was that all these folks were

aware of the local oddball stuff, but they couldn't think of it. Why? Because they saw these things every day. The oddities were part of the daily wallpaper. In a coffee shop in Bryant, Indiana, the server told me that there wasn't much to see in town. But twenty minutes later, just a quarter mile from the shop, I drove past a barn adorned with hundreds of monkey wrenches that had been nailed to the side of the building. I returned to the café on the way out of town. "Oh, I forgot about that," said the embarrassed waitress, who had drawn a blank when I'd posed the original question an hour earlier.

Writing the book required a lot of poking around. On many occasions my search required engaging a total stranger in an interview. Outside central Indiana, no one knew my face or had heard of my dog. But Barney played a role similar to the one he played in Indy. He greased relationships and helped me to gain the trust of perfect strangers, whom I was asking to share their story. In the rural Midwest most people have gun racks, not ski racks, so I was glad have a beagle next to me. Not for protection, for a connection.

In Knox, Indiana, northwest of Indianapolis, the first six people I spoke with at a gas station, all from the immediate neighborhood, failed to remember that one of their neighbors had giant rosary beads encircling her house. They were multi-colored *bowling balls*, connected by a rope. In fact, everyone in Knox knew about this oddity, but again, unless I specifically mentioned it, the locals were at a loss to think of anything in town that would make it into my book.

When I found the address, I whipped out my camera and starting snapping photos. I would normally have asked permission, but it appeared no one was home. Suddenly, an elderly woman emerged from the house. At first she appeared distressed at my picture taking, although you would think I wasn't the first person to see this as a Kodak moment. "Can I help you?" she asked cautiously. I explained I was writing a book about unique things in Indiana. "Oh, do you think I'll get in the book?"

"Yes, ma'am."

She was genuinely flattered but reluctant to grant permission, concerned I might mock her house. Barney had stuck his head out the window and was howling for some attention. "Is that your dog?"

"Yes, his name is Barney."

"I had beagles when I was growing up. Why don't you two come in the house and I'll tell you the whole story of my rosary."

Barney and I had a lovely visit, sharing beagle stories with the owner of the house, Linda Stage. She also provided a fascinating history of her unique rosary beads, leaving little to spare, so to speak. Like most Hoosiers, the inclination was to be open and friendly, but it sometimes required a little evidence on my part that I was to be trusted.

We left an hour later with story in hand. That chapter of the book always created the most interest. Barney helped make that happen.

When the book came out, one reviewer noted, "Dick has fun with people, but he doesn't make fun of them." I appreciated the distinction, but sometimes I did have to gnaw on my lip. I did seem to meet some unique personalities.

By the way, Barney always enjoyed the ride through rural Indiana, his head out the window, nose twitching. He was a real trouper. And sometimes there were state troopers following our car, but I never got a speeding ticket in all the years I drove through Indiana if Barney was with me. And I was stopped more than a few times. Without Barney, I'd have had a few citations. Yeah, the dog even melted the hearts of Indiana's finest.

Barney often looked back over his shoulder as we passed fields of cows and sheep. I'm sure Barney would have liked to have made a few unscheduled stops, but there were just too many curiosities to sniff out. We were on a deadline.

Walk a Mile in My Paws

Barney and I qualified for senior citizenship about the same time. I was the oldest on-air reporter at WISH-TV. I hadn't been there the longest, but I was the longest in the tooth. Now I was dying the hair that had been success-fully transplanted from one part of my head to another years earlier. At fifty-three years old, I wasn't quite as enthusiastic about segments that involved a bodily commitment. I had had enough of roller skating, acrobatic plane rides, and bear wrestling. In the past, I had jumped at every opportunity to be physically involved in the segment. Viewers always loved those parts of the show. But now there were parts of me that needed a rest. One thing that remained a constant was my daily walk with Barney. We both would head out the door, although sometimes I thought the pooch would rather have curled up on the air conditioner vent and slept. I often felt the same way.

We usually started out at a good pace. I'd lumber for about five minutes, at which point both my heart and the dog's reached peak cardiac rate. Both of us were about 15 percent over our optimum body weight, so it wasn't long before the two us were tripping over our tongues.

The once-three-mile jaunt became barely a mile. In the summer, I'd bring a spray bottle when it was over 75 degrees, and every tenth of a mile or so we'd sit on a rock and refresh ourselves. In the winter, we'd both bundle up in sweaters before we left the house, but within an hour all six of our feet were freezing and needed a good rub.

Both Barney and I had arthritis as we aged. And it couldn't have come at a better time. When Barney was younger, he would get the scent of a rabbit and take off into the woods. Even then, I couldn't keep up with a beagle pup. Once Barney reached about eleven, he'd still eye the squirrels and rabbits, but I think even he realized that pursuit would be in vain. He didn't make an effort anymore. Sometimes I'd catch a glimpse of an attractive young woman in the park. Barney and I would look at each other knowingly. Who were we kidding?

We still enjoyed the trees and wildlife, but we both developed allergies in late summer, so we'd trudge down the trail sneezing and wheezing. In the winter, we walked gingerly along the icy streets, afraid we might slip and twist one our six ankles or whatever they're called on a dog.

On a typical walk, Barney relieved himself fifteen or twenty times. Even if I were inclined to do likewise, propriety (and having a recognizable face) prevented me from following suit, but I wouldn't have minded a few pit stops myself.

As our walk came to an end, we'd both be panting, looking forward to the ride home when we could both stick our heads out the window and let the wind run through our thinning and graying hairs. Once we arrived at the house, Barney headed right for his bowl of cold water. I'd snap open a frosty beer and before long we were both napping on the sofa. That's usually when my wife got home from work and thought it funny to point out that the dog and I snored in perfect harmony.

I never put Barney on a leash when we walked in the woods. Over the years, this had proven to be a mistake. A rabbit or squirrel would send him scampering and the result was that I often had to depend on pure luck that he would find his way back to me. He usually did, but on more than a few occasions, I would search for more than an hour, calling him at the top of my voice to no avail. When I finally returned home without him, there was usually a phone call on my answering machine from somebody who had found him sniffing about in his garage. In later years, he stuck closer to me. As I said, we had both lost a little wanderlust.

I estimated once that the two of us walked about 4,000 miles together. More than anything else, more even than our time on TV, I miss those walks. There were no fans to please, no news directors to satisfy, no time cues to hit, no makeup to put on.

I'm not a tree hugger or a nature nut. I'm just a city boy who moved west from New York and discovered that a half hour in the woods with your best friend is even sweeter than a half-sour pickle.

Grow Old Along with Me

The earliest sign of Barney's aging was the gradual loss of his hearing. Those big droopy ears could once detect a Pringle hitting the kitchen floor at thirty paces. Barney could hear me crack a dog biscuit three rooms away. He knew the doorbell was going to ring seconds before it chimed—he heard the footsteps. When Barney was deep in the woods behind our house, I'd rattle a box of Milk-Bones and he would be at the back door in seconds. But his personal radar system was going on the fritz. Those big ears were becoming just so much window dressing.

Maybe I should have identified this problem earlier. Commands like "Come here!" "Sit!" "Bad dog!" "Stop eating trash!" went unheeded. But since he'd never paid any attention to those commands when he had perfect hearing, I didn't realize what was happening.

Barney and I did about 2,500 shows together. Mornings went like this: I'd switch off the alarm, jump in the shower, and get dressed. Waiting for me at the door half an hour later was Barney, ready for a new adventure. But one day, he wasn't at the door; he was still curled up in my bed, snoring away. He hadn't heard the alarm, or the shower, or the flushing toilet. He was shaking and vibrating in the middle of some doggy fantasy dream. I hated to wake him up. But we had to go to work.

For years, when the family went out for the day, Barney would spend his afternoon on our bed, his head propped against my pillow, body stretched out like a lazy feline. When we'd return, he'd hear the car pull into the driveway and dash downstairs to greet us at the door.

No more.

I walked into the bedroom, where he was snoozing. I tried to roust him by bellowing his name. *Barney! Barney, we're home.*

No response.

I walked over and gently scratched his belly. His head snapped up like a jack-in-the-box. *"What in blazes was that?"* he seemed to be saying. *"You scared me half to death."* Like most dogs, and especially beagles, Barney was used to hearing it or smelling it before he saw it or felt it. Now I felt bad when I disturbed him. *Maybe,* I thought, *I should call home and say we're on the way . . .* not that he would have heard the phone. Or knew how to answer it.

Our walks in the woods changed, as well. Beagles are hounds, bred to travel in packs when they hunt. Barney often walked ahead of me but would on occasion twist his head around to be sure I was nearby, still part of the hunting party. But such confirmation was rare because he could hear my footsteps. On occasion, I would hide behind a tree. When the footsteps stopped, he predictably turned to check my where-abouts. This confirmed his devotion to me, a method that has never worked with my wife, who once walked ahead of me for a half mile while I hid behind a tree.

My walk with Barney was changing. He didn't hear my footsteps anymore, so he'd waddle along with his body almost at right angles, bent in the middle, so he could see me at every step. He looked as though he had a perpetual stiff neck years old. If he turned and looked ahead, he'd have no evidence I was following him.

He could still smell a doughnut a block away and he remained bright-eyed and alert, even for almost thirteen years old. If you saw Barney at an event, you couldn't tell his ears had failed him. It didn't matter, he could still feel the love: Isn't he cute? Isn't he adorable? Isn't he precious? I sometimes wondered if he could read lips.

I'd known and loved Barney for a dozen years, but since I'd found him by my front door, I never knew his exact age. It was one of the questions I had to field throughout his our television careers.

"How old is he?"

I'm not sure how many times I answered that question over the years. Not about me. About Barney. My answer changed every year, of course. Inquiries about my age, however, required a more consistent response. Heck, I said I was *about* fifty for more than a decade.

Each November when we made personal appearances at the local holiday gift and hobby show, I'd print up a sign with Barney's age so I did not have to repeat the answer to literally thousands of fans who started each conversation this way.

Naturally, I did get other questions, and some downright bizarre ones over the years.

"Is Barney his real name?"

No, his real name is Alan, but we changed it because it just doesn't work on TV.

"Is Barney your dog?"

No, he's a rental. Pet him quick. He's due back in an hour.

Honestly, I resisted those snappy retorts because they could suggest a lack of respect for the questioner, often just a sincere fan who wanted to make conversation. I was torn between the comic Dick Wolfsie and the pet lover Dick Wolfsie, Barney's dad.

As Barney grew in stature (both in fame and fat) I started hearing things like, "Whoa, he's getting up there in years," and "How's ol' Barn doing?" But the worst was, "Dick, what are you going to do when he's gone?"

Despite the hearing loss, Barney still remained ornery and mischievous, the two qualities that allowed him to keep his competitive edge as a TV talent.

Brett was now in middle school and less bothered by Barney's distractive behavior, but still not a fan. Three quarters of Brett's life, as far back as his memory would take him, there had been a Barney. This tarnished and then cemented his view of all canines as needy, destructive competitors. To this day, my son—now an adult—doesn't warm easily to dogs. How ironic that this self-professed cat lover hailed from a family whose dog stole the hearts of everyone else in central Indiana.

Mary Ellen had become the reluctant admirer, now sensing that his days were numbered and recognizing what an impact he had made on Indianapolis. And our own lives. She remained until the end Barney's mom, a mantle she once wore unwillingly, but now wore as a badge of honor, like a military hero tested in combat.

Barney had never had a sick day in his life until his final years. Other than two nasty bites out of his butt, both by a couple of pugnacious pugs we encountered on a leisurely walk in the woods, his hearty beagle nature generally kept him away from the vet except for normal checkups. Save those few places he was clearly not allowed (and there weren't many) and the one place I knew petrified him—the ice rink at Market Square arena, where he could never get his footing—he never missed a show. Not to brag, but I never missed a show myself. Like anyone ever noticed.

But then Barney started to gain even more additional weight. I knew something was wrong. Bob McCune, Barney's regular doc, suggested I see a veterinary internist in Anderson, Indiana, who was part of a well-known clinic run by the state's top animal orthopedist. But Dr. McCune also warned that specialists were inclined to suggest some rather heroic techniques that I might not be comfortable with.

I had taken Barney there once when I thought his tail had been caught in a door. The happy appendage had stopped wagging, a clear sign that Barney was suffering. Dr. Lee had X-rayed the tail and confirmed there had been a minor fracture.

"Does it hurt him?" I asked.

"It's like impotence," explained the vet. "Painless but humiliating."

Needless to say, his tail healed. And wagged uninterruptedly for many years.

At the clinic, the internist ran some preliminary tests, then provided me with an entire list of options I could consider to better pinpoint the diagnosis. Many of the tests were intrusive. And expensive. Money was not the issue, but Barney had reached the stage where I believed that the entire ordeal would just result in a potential short extension of his life. And who was I doing that for—him or me?

I opted for a few of the procedures, primarily to rule out one disorder that was quite treatable. When the tests came back, so did a bombshell. Barney had a possible abscess on one of his kidneys and the specialist was suggesting that it be removed. Not the abscess, the kidney. I listened to her rationale but was unconvinced. This was a twelve-year-old dog suffering no apparent pain and still pleased as puppy chow to accompany me every day and do his thing.

The next day I went to see Dr. McCune, who agreed that it was a quality-of-life issue. The trauma of the surgery coupled with a tough recovery period dissuaded me from the dramatic procedure that was being recommended.

Going home in the car, I pulled over to the side of the road and gave Barney a hug, as I often did when we faced a mutual problem. "I think we made the right decision, ol' buddy."

The thought of his death, and life without Barney, was something I did not do a lot of thinking about. I had heard that Bob and Tom, hosts of a nationally syndicated radio show that originated in Indianapolis, had large insurance policies on each other's lives, protecting them and their families against financial loss if one of the partners died. How clever that was, but probably not something even Lloyd's of London would do for a guy and his dog. My life insurance agent was a good friend, but this was not a call I was going to make.

Heavenly Bed

Our twelfth appearance at the Indiana State Fair began with a beastly hot morning that would only get muggier as the day went on. A few days earlier we had reported live from the balloon race, where, as always, the governor stopped by for a quick interview.

We had invited a representative of the Westin Hotel chain to unveil their Heavenly Bed for Dogs, part of a campaign for the chain to promote traveling with pets.

Even now when I look at the videotape, I still marvel at how Barney always knew exactly what to do to make the segment work, how to make the audience laugh. How to make people say, "What a dog!"

The segment began with a quick explanation of the Westin's decision to allow guests to bring their dogs to their hotel when on vacation, then ended with the first public display of the three-foot-square white poofy cushion that was provided to travelers for their pets. I thought it kind of ironic at the time. If the Westin was going to encourage people to bring destructive dogs like Barney to their hotel, the concept didn't have much of a chance to succeed, which, by the way, it didn't. They ended the program not long after. I never heard officially why, but the word was that allowing people to have dogs in the hotel room and encouraging them to do so was a line they shouldn't have crossed. And a room they didn't want to clean.

As soon as the hotel manager placed the pillow on the ground, Barney, who had been otherwise distracted by about a million State Fair odors, made a beeline for the cushion, sniffed it for a few seconds, then proceeded to roll over on his back and fall asleep belly up . . . all in about twenty seconds, just before we went to a commercial break. "I don't think I could afford that kind of advertising," said the general manager of the Westin. "How'd you get him to do that?"

I knew that the rest of that day was going to be difficult for the aging hound. After the morning show, we returned home so both of us could enjoy our daily nap, a custom that had spanned our entire career together.

The routine was standard: I'd grab a book, prop up two pillows against the headboard in my room, then lie back and begin to read. Barney would rest his head on my stomach. In ninety seconds we were both sound asleep. With that method, it took me three years to read *Tuesdays with Morrie*.

The plan that day was to return for the State Fair celebrity parade, an annual event that featured most of the WISH-TV personalities. Barney had been in nine of these events, always outshining the newsmen and newswomen who never quite garnered the same fan response from the crowd.

"Barney! I watch you every day!"

"Wow, it's Barney!"

"Look, there's Barney!"

He reveled in every minute of it as we rumbled down the main drag at the fair in a wagon pulled by a green John Deere tractor. I held him in my lap, propping him up so the masses could clearly see him, often taking his paw and waving it to the crowd. The other Channel 8 on-air personalities waved as well. As many admitted later, all eyes were on Barney.

Once the parade was over, though, I had a problem. The temperature was nearing 90 and I had a book signing and tickets to watch Garrison Keillor that night at the Fairgrounds Coliseum. Even with the brief respite at home, I knew I was pushing the old guy.

One of the WISH-TV staffers, marketing director Carol Sergi, sensed my concern, so she offered to drop Barney at my house on her way home around 5:30. Barney was clearly feeling the effects of the weather and I knew he'd be glad to be taxied back to the air-conditioned house. But I still wasn't overly concerned with his present condition. There was a huge crowd at the fair that evening—and more cows, pigs, and horses than you could shake a shovel at. Overall, everyone seemed to be coping with the heat and humidity.

I attended the Keillor concert and even had a chance to meet him backstage before the show, then found my seat and was thrilled to be sitting right behind Governor O'Bannon and his wife, Judy. We exchanged hellos and they asked how Barney was doing. Toward the end of the event, I snuck out a little early, hoping to beat the exiting crowd. I also wanted to get home in time to bathe Barney. He had spent a few minutes that day in the cow barn with me and had enjoyed the aromatic benefits of rolling in manure.

I found my SUV in the giant infield lot and negotiated it out onto the main highway, then headed toward my house. My cell phone rang.

"It's Barney," my wife said. "There's something wrong."

"I'll be right home." I hung up. I jammed on the accelerator. The cell phone rang one more time. It was Mary Ellen again: "Don't have an accident. It's too late. He's gone. Barney is gone. Please be careful. There is nothing you can do."

I banged my wrists against the steering wheel. I wanted it to hurt. I wanted to feel something. I couldn't find the tears. Not yet. I remember saying, "Oh, God! Oh, God! Oh, God!"

How odd to talk to yourself like that. Even then, I knew how strange it was. My life is performing in front of people. But there was no audience there. Just me. In a car. Alone. I was still ten miles from what would be one of the most difficult moments of my life.

For the next several minutes, all was just a blur. I knew he had not suffered, and that I had avoided the unthinkable: the prospect of someday putting him "down." I missed him already. Damn. I wasn't with him at the end. Then more questions. Could I have done something? What would I do tomorrow without him? What would I do ... from now on?

I shot into the driveway, slammed on the brakes, shut off the car, and barreled up the stairs to the extra bedroom where Barney always napped. I'm not sure why I hurried. It was over. The inevitable had happened. Barney the beagle, my best friend, my business partner, was gone.

The Heavenly Bed spot was Barney's final TV appearance. Would I have wanted to know that this was the last time our viewers would see him and the last time the two of us would be a team? Or did I want to enjoy that Barney moment in the same way I had enjoyed the thousands before it? In the end, I was glad for the latter. I also knew that if Barney could have planned his last day, it would have been at the State Fair: 50,000 people, hundreds of smells. He didn't have to die that day. He was already in heaven.

I picked him up, draped him over my shoulder, buried my head in his neck, and sobbed. Mary Ellen stroked Barney while I held him. Brett just kept staring at me. He had never seen me cry. This frightened him. I remember the first time I saw my father weep. It made him seem more human than I ever realized. I doubt Brett was truly saddened by Barney's passing, but he grieved for me. He must have wondered what this event would mean, what effect it would have on the family. I wondered, too.

Then I asked Mary Ellen and Brett to give me a few minutes alone with Barney. I just hugged him and hugged him.

For most of the evening, I lay on the guest bed with him next to me. Finally, around midnight, I fell asleep. Morning for me was only four hours away.

It's human nature that when you fall asleep, burdened by some horrible event, there is that fleeting hope that when you awaken the next morning, it will have all been a dream—that somehow a new day will bring a fresh perspective, and with it, the ability to rewind the tape and do some fancy editing. Not so, and just hours later, I got up, wrapped Barney in a blanket, and placed him in his doggie bed. Then I headed for work. That's right, for work.

I was scheduled to do my regular TV remote at the State Fair, a segment with Howard Helmer, officially known as the world's fastest omelet maker. At that point, I had no choice but to do the show. There was no viable way to cancel a live segment at the last minute.

Howard was a great guest who had achieved record-breaking notoriety in his career by preparing 427 of his egg dishes in under thirty minutes. "Very wet ones," he'd often admit. Howard and I had been doing television together for twenty-five years, starting back at my early TV days in

Columbus. Howard's snappy comments during his demos made him the ultimate talk-show guest. After completing an omelet, he'd present his masterpiece to the crowd and declare its approximate menu value: "$2.95," he'd say, to a smattering of applause. Then he'd place a sprig of parsley next to his creation: "$6.95," he'd deadpan. Big laugh. Even from me, and I had heard it thirty times.

I met my photographer, Carl Finchum, at the fairgrounds and we exchanged our customary good mornings. Carl was not a 5 a.m. kind of person, so I suspected that he would not pick up on what I assumed was a transparent change in my demeanor. I was a morning person, a quality that annoyed my wife and many other people. Most of my guests assumed my generosity of spirit at dawn was a charade. It wasn't. I liked mornings. Except this one.

My plan was not to share the previous night's events with anyone, convinced that verbalizing my grief would result in a total breakdown. It had taken me a good three hours the night before to compose myself, and now I was about twenty minutes from persuading tens of thousands of people watching the show that you could make a presentable spinach and cheddar cheese omelet in less than sixty seconds. This would have to be an Oscar-winning performance.

Suddenly Howard appeared with his entourage, a flock of volunteers from the Indiana Poultry Association who were also committed to Howard's egg-promoting mission. Howard and I exchanged hugs. Turns out he was good at reading embraces.

"What's the matter?"

"Nothing, nothing. Just a bad night."

"Are you sure? You seem . . . different."

"No. I'm fine."

"Where's Barney?"

"Oh, he was up late last night at the fair. I let him sleep in."

And so, I had told my first whopper. More to come. I had a whole weekend ahead of me: book signings, a speech, dinner with friends. I had no idea how I would spin the events.

I also realized I had to make the necessary arrangements. Despite my awareness of Barney's age and illness, I had given no thought—zero—to where his final resting place would be. Cremation was a possibility and available through most veterinarians, but I had never been comfortable with this choice for either man or beast, so I nixed that option.

There was a pet cemetery in town, but somehow that was terribly wrong. I wanted Barney near me, like he had been for almost thirteen years. And Barney was a people-dog, not a dog-dog. Other dogs were never a real kick for Barney. At dog parks and on trails, he gravitated toward humans, hardly giving the other dogs a sniff. Dogs didn't have pockets with treats. It was always an easy choice: people over pooches. And so, I didn't want to stick him in between a lot of strangers almost an hour from my house. Home was where the hound would be, I decided. That was my decision and both Mary Ellen and Brett agreed.

Burying an animal in your backyard is forbidden by Indiana code, but I was never a big fan of rules. A few friends said something about the law being health related, but the woods behind our house had the carcass of a dead deer, and when I had reported that to the city months earlier, they didn't seem to care enough to do anything about it. What a stupid law. I chose to ignore it.

Marking the final site was the easiest part of the final arrangements and it had, believe it or not, been determined years earlier. I had done a segment at a local funeral home in 1995 where they offered laser-engraved tombstones that not only had the person's name, but the deceased's image, as well.

Originally the show was booked with the idea that the artist would make a stone for Barney's ultimate gravesite, a real eventuality, but it struck me at the time to be so far in the future. We made it very clear on the segment that this funeral home did not cater to pet owners and this was just a demonstration. That didn't stop thirty people from calling about their pets. People hear what they want to hear.

Barney's image was engraved onto the 20 × 20-inch piece of marble as tens of thousands watched the process. It was a little spooky, but again, another opportunity to insert Barney into the show content. Now I had a gravestone when Barney died. I'd kept it hidden in the basement because the daily sight of it creeped me out. I thought of that marble stone as I held Barney in my arms that night.

The question of what sort of container I should use for his body troubled me. He deserved a wooden box, but a canine coffin was not something you can put your finger on at a moment's notice. Instead, I simply wrapped him in one of my bedsheets, a sheet he had probably spent more than a few thousand hours sleeping on.

Saturday morning, Brett and I went out to the back of the house to dig the grave. Our backyard was rocky with hundreds of trees, which meant that if you dug just a few inches down, you'd run smack into a root system. The tears flowed and Brett, who had warmed to Barney near the end, put his arm around my shoulder and reminded me what a great life I had given Barney—and he had given me.

At that moment, I saw a change in Brett. He was older and was no longer dealing with the same issues that had confronted him as a toddler when Dad's pet destroyed his toys and competed for his parents' attention. I don't think he ever developed a true affection for Barney, but he finally realized how much he had meant to me and all the people who watched him every day.

"Everybody loved him, didn't they, Dad?" They sure did, Brett. They sure did.

Once I had buried Barney and covered him with dirt, I leaned the headstone against a nearby tree. More tears. More even than the night he died.

I decided then that his burial spot would be a secret, a decision motivated by my reading Laura Hillebrand's book, *Seabiscuit*. The Howard family, owners of the famous race-horse, did not want the interment to be made public. Both Seabiscuit and Barney were unlikely stars who had touched an entire community. But some things, said the Howards, needed to remain private. I agreed. Plus, Barney was now buried *illegally*. More grief I didn't need.

I have now shared this secret with you. I'm sure it is safe.

That weekend I did a couple of book signings and side-stepped the inevitable inquiries from fans: How's Barney? Where's Barney? I gave a speech that night to a local Chamber of Commerce and peppered the presentation with funny Barney stories. His non-appearance at evening events was understood, especially at dinners where his lack of self-control around food was funny for about five minutes, then downright annoying.

But why the deception? I wasn't sure. I did know that what was a distinctly personal tragedy in my life had some real consequences in central Indiana. Blurting it out, even to close friends and colleagues that morning, would have meant that soon it would become evident that I had somehow managed to soldier my way through an omelet demo just hours after central Indiana's favorite canine had died. Sure, some people would say that was the professional in me. The other 98 percent would think I was a callous jerk. Even I wasn't sure which was more accurate.

I didn't sleep at all that weekend. I just stared into space. I had lost my best friend. I had lost my business partner.

It was probably a full week before an overwhelming sense of guilt hit me. I questioned every decision I made the day he died. Should I have realized the day was too hot for him? Should I have brought him back for the parade? Did I really have to go to see Garrison Keillor that night?

I shared all this with close friends and, of course, Mary Ellen. Needless to say, they all thought I was silly to feel any responsibility for his death, but the hurt cut so deep that I was almost immobilized. That's all I thought about.

That Monday I told our news director of Barney's death. Tom Cochrun had been on the job for exactly one day. He was a former investigative reporter–turned anchor–turned documentary producer. He enjoyed a good reputation and was an old friend. He had taken over for former director Lee Giles in order to reinvent the WISH-TV news presentation, which some felt needed a makeover.

For almost a year I had been aware that things were a-changin' in local TV news. The tragedy of 9/11 had led to some research suggesting that local TV viewers didn't have time for nonessential viewing. Weather, traffic, and local news drove the ratings. Warm, fuzzy stories and human interest pieces might work in the early evening when people were home and settled in for the night, but they were just an interruption in the AM when people needed to gulp down their coffee and get to work. This research was not a good sign for guys like me who did fun stuff.

Cochrun was appropriately sympathetic when I told him, but I don't think this was what he wanted to deal with on his first day. Of course, you can never predict what will happen in news. So this was good training for him. He made no statement or reference to my acquiring another dog. I suppose that made sense, lest he be accused of being insensitive and thinking only of the commercial value of the next "Barney." As I walked out the door, I was confused as to what was next. Another dog? Another job?

Cochrun released the information to the paper on Tuesday and the news spread quickly. Pam Elliot, the morning anchor, was assigned the task of doing a feature on Barney's life and Debbie Knox, the veteran anchor, reported the event as a news story that evening. In both accounts we played the more famous clips, including his rosebush incident and the coon-dog competition.

The *Indianapolis Star* ran a front-page story titled "The Little Bandit Is Dead," and the story came with an apology from the writer, who phoned to tell me that she had written a more detailed account of Barney's life and influence, but her boss didn't quite get it. "Why would we write that much about a dog?" he asked her. The *Star* at the time had undergone many changes including a huge influx of editors from the Gannett newspaper chain who did not know the city.

The phone rang all night. E-mails piled in, more than 500 by 10 PM Dozens of floral bouquets showed up on my doorstep and at the studio. Two days later, my mailbox at WISH-TV was crammed with cards and letters of condolence. Truly astonishing in this age when dashing off something at the computer is the easiest way to communicate. People even sent dog biscuits. *Huh?* By the end of the week, I had more than 3,000 e-mails, including one from AOL asking what was going on. Had I been spammed to death?

At first I tried to answer every correspondence. The task was monumental, and finally I realized that I couldn't spend the next two weeks in the basement responding to every well-wisher. Every now and then, I occasionally run into people who did get one of my few thank-you notes, and their gratitude is so sincere I have some regrets that I did not finish the task.

Most people were doing more than expressing condolences; they were sharing a personal story of their own losses. Barney's passing was an opportunity to vent these feelings. And it wasn't always about a pet. For some, grieving over Barney helped deal with memories of family, parents, and siblings. Some of the letters were hard to read because they were so intensely personal from people I had never met. Yes, they felt as though they knew me and could share what they had gone through in a similar situation.

Almost every fan had a favorite Barney memory. I was struck at how different segments had tickled different people, occasionally even reminding me of a show that I had long since forgotten. "Dick, do you remember the time Barney got his nose stuck on the dry ice?" Actually, I had forgotten all about that. Thanks for the memory.

Viewers had been touched by Barney, amused by him, maybe even had food stolen by him—and they wanted me to know it. As much as I had come to understand Barney's celebrity, I now fully appreciated the emotional attachment people had to him. I have the letters. I've read them. And wept.

Friends, colleagues, and fans also shared their feelings about my getting a new dog. Some felt that a replacement would mend my broken heart and repair a professional set-back. But should it be a beagle? "No," said many. "There will never be another Barney." "He will remind you too much of Barney." "It would be an insult to Barney." Others urged me to find another beagle. Only then, they said, could I fill the void.

Barney's appearance on TV at 5 AM, or whenever in the morning you first tuned in, was a signal for the day to start. Car crashes, murders, floods, scams, all the stations covered that stuff. But for tens of thousands of people every morning, the little brown and white and black menace was the official beginning of the day. Hundreds of my e-mails began: "I can't start my morning until I see Barney" or "It takes a little mischief to get my adrenaline going." I was struck by the depth of the emotion. These were not just fans: they were more like converts to some kind of beagle cult.

Many of the letters shared favorite moments, personal interactions with Barney, usually at a public appearance. "You won't remember me, but I held Barney at the Tipton Library while you made a speech. He got in my purse and ate half my lipstick." "I walked Barney at the fair while you were selling books." "Hey, Dick. I rescued Barney from the thorn bushes once."

With all the grief I was feeling, I still felt guilt about how I had pushed Barney his final day at the fair. A letter from animal behavior expert Dr. Gary Sampson finally eased the pain.

I had not heard from Gary since the day on my front porch nine years earlier when Barney had gnawed through the microphone cable and uprooted the rosebushes during Dr. Sampson's explanation of how to cure destructive behavior in dogs.

"I will always remember Barney and what a neat dog he was," said Dr. Sampson. "And how special for both of you that he should have spent his final day just as he lived his whole life, in front of the people he loved and those who loved him."

***

I still have every e-mail and letter—several thousand of them—and I reread most of them in preparation for writing this book. Had I exaggerated in my own mind how much he was loved? Not a bit. But if I had to pick one public acknowledgment of how Barney affected people, it would be the billboard a local veterinarian placed outside his clinic. He was not Barney's doctor, just a fan. I saw it quite by accident as I drove by a few days after I buried my sidekick.

GOODBYE, BARNEY,
WE WILL MISS YOU

I pulled over to the side of the road. I didn't cry. Instead, I had a huge grin on my face. For the next hour.

On live TV the first morning after his death was announced, I acknowledged the condolences of the *Daybreak* team but did not make any attempt to relate the events of the previous days, in part because I had spun a story related to the date of his death. But also because I feared that I would break down emotionally prior to the beginning of the next segment. That night I went home and wrote this column for local newspapers.

Goodbye, Barney

I lost my best friend this week. And my business partner. Barney was 12 or 13 or 14. I never really knew his exact age. He was a street kid who wandered onto my doorstep looking for a better life. He found it. And I found the world's greatest dog.

I'm not going to tell you exactly when Barney died because after it happened I lied to dozens of people. You might be one of them. "Where's Barney?" they yelled from their car the next day. "Home sleeping," I shot back. I didn't know what words to use. He wasn't just my dog that was gone. He was their dog. In many ways, Barney belonged to everyone.

When I walked down the street with him, four out of five people would say hello to the beagle by name. Many followed with a lame joke about not knowing my name. Sometimes they weren't kidding.

There was never another dog like him. He was a dog with many passions. People would joke that he looked like he hadn't missed many meals. I think he missed one, back near the millennium. He was endlessly hungry, relentlessly in a search for food he could steal. He ate everything: pickles, carrots, hot dog buns, tomatoes. And sometimes, when extremely desperate, he would eat his own dog food.

When he saw people approach in a mall, he rolled over on his back for the ultimate belly rub. If you stopped rubbing him, he glared at you. "You've got some nerve," he seemed to be saying. Everyone rubbed his belly—little old ladies, toddlers, Harley riders, even cat lovers.

As much as he loved me, he'd run away if he had the chance. Not run away from me, but on to a new adventure. He knew I'd find him. Last Thanksgiving he got through the invisible fence and found his way to a holiday dinner several miles away. He barked at the unfamiliar door. He knew strangers were a softer touch at the dinner table.

Barney and I did 3,000 TV shows together on Channel 8.

Barney knew television.

When a second-rate musician was playing his electric guitar on my show, Barney pulled the plug out of the wall with his teeth.

Barney knew music.

When the new Ruth's Chris opened downtown, Barney went into the kitchen during the show and stole a T-bone from the counter.

Barney knew steak.

When Barney was asleep, his tail actually wagged.

Barney knew how to dream.

When I did a show with kids with Down syndrome, Barney jumped on the bed with all ten toddlers and snuggled with them.

Barney knew how to love.

When I did a show with the Carmel High School baseball team, he stole the ball (and the show) and took off with the whole squad in hot pursuit.

Barney knew comedy.

When people took pictures of Barney, I swear he looked right at the camera.

Barney knew publicity.

Barney loved everyone. There were no strangers. I don't think he had an unhappy moment in his life. His final day was filled with good food and adoring fans. That evening he passed peacefully, I am convinced.

Barney even knew how to die.

Over the years, I have given out over 5,000 photos of Barney, each inscribed by me with a silly facsimile of a paw print. If you have a picture of Barney with that paw print, please keep it in his memory. That would mean a lot to me.

And, I am sure, it would mean a lot to Barney.

A few days after that column appeared, an e-mail was sent to staff by the general manager—interestingly, one that I never got—instructing station employees not to respond to any inquiries from the press, or from viewers for that matter, about whether there would be a replacement for Barney. At first glance, I was perplexed by the memo when a colleague showed it to me because I had already responded during my interview with the local anchor, making it clear that the hunt would soon commence for a new sidekick. Worse, the local paper, the *Indianapolis Star*, had run a front-page feature about Barney's demise and had quoted me as saying there would be another beagle at some point. Had I stuck my paw in my mouth?

So what did this edict mean? Well, if the station was smart, it would milk this situation for all it was worth. Newspaper ads, station promotion, Humane Society involvement, more Barney look-alike contests. This was going to be big: who will be the next Barney?

But that's not what the e-mail was implying. That's not what my gut had told me for two years, ever since 9/11. Instead, it appeared I was getting a subtle signal that the dog days of WISH-TV were over. That the morning news would no longer be identified by a renegade little beagle who had captured the hearts of every single viewer. The station felt it was time to move on.

I have no idea how many lives Barney touched. Every morning in front of their TV sets tens of thousands of people anticipated his appearance and were primed to smile and head out for work. When they arrived at the office or the factory, they delivered a Channel 8 commercial: "Did you see *Daybreak* today? You will not believe what Barney did." "Did you see him chew that boxing glove?" "Can you believe he ate an entire plate of lasagna?"

Barney met the needs of each person he encountered. Everybody who ever hugged Barney, or scratched his belly or his ears, connected with him. This is not some romantic notion. I have heard the stories, seen the response. I watched the dog do his thing. And he did it so well that I really believe he was one of a kind.

Canines differ in temperament and mood, so clearly some dogs could not have played a TV role. But there are packs of pooches out there who are as loving and charming as Barney was. Could another dog, had he shown up on my steps, have been a Barney? Good question.

Matchmaker, Matchmaker

In the weeks after Barney's passing, I felt like half of Indiana was suddenly in the matchmaking business. Everybody had a friend who had an extra beagle, or had found a beagle, or knew somebody who knew somebody who'd just had four of the cutest, most adorable beagle puppies you ever saw and I better act now or they might give them to the pound, where they might be put to sleep. Please, spare me. Things were tough enough.

I resisted most overtures, but some were tough to ignore. I received several calls from two local humane societies and paid them the courtesy of a visit, just to look at the beagles up for adoption. I knew the possible fate of many of these dogs, which was just crushing for me, but none of them looked like Barney. Why should that have mattered? For some reason, I felt no connection to these dogs. The color was wrong, the howl was off, the wag wavered. Too short, too thin. Lack of sufficient floppiness in the ears. The eyes weren't right. Man, those eyes. That was the deal breaker. No one had eyes like Barney. Right into his soul. And into mine.

There was one beagle, Stanley, at the Hamilton County Humane Society, who did catch my attention. And he looked like Barney, but *he* was a girl. Yes, a girl named Stanley. And for reasons that I cannot explain but will probably get me in trouble with feminists, this was not a female role I was casting. I wanted a Jim Carrey, not a Tina Fey. I know that's totally nuts. But that's how I felt.

One afternoon when I was at my computer writing a newspaper column, the phone rang . . . "Mr. Wolfsie, you don't know me, but I'm down at the shopping center about three minutes from where you live and I drove two hours to show you my six beagle puppies. It would be an honor if you would put one on TV and make him a star."

I jumped in the car to take a look. How could I not? The dogs were adorable. So adorable, in fact, that while I was playing with them in this huge pen, people in the parking lot recognized me and thought they were about to witness a historic event: the selection of the new Barney. I resisted taking one of the pups, but I am pleased to say that three of the dogs found a home that day.

One of the complications of my decision was that our cat Lindsay, who was within a whisker of twenty-one years old, was in no condition to deal with a new dog. I made a promise—no new dog while Lindsay was still alive—to my wife, and that took the pressure off me to continue the search. Mary Ellen was happy being beagle-less, at least temporarily.

Two weeks later, Lindsay retreated to the laundry room and as cats often do, passed away quietly in private. She was a classy cat who never gave a mouse's ass about Barney. Over the dozen years, there was an occasional swat and maybe one or two hisses, but Lindsay was unimpressed with the TV star. That's how cats are.

Our other cat, Benson, still spry at nineteen, might have to face the prospect of a new housemate. I knew he wouldn't like it. Well, tough.

Then in September, just six weeks after Barney died, a call from a former guest, just one of thousands on my show who had been moved by Barney's death. Marcia had two loves: dogs and mushrooms. She had been on *Daybreak* twice, each time highlighting her business, Fungus Amongus, an endeavor that made her a favorite with local chefs who prized her home-grown mold. To quote her T-shirt: SHIITAKE HAPPENS.

"I have a dog I want you to see. A beagle. I've had him for a couple of weeks. A stray."

"Marcia, please don't do this to me."

"Dick. You have to see this dog."

Marcia knew mushrooms, but she also knew dogs. She was harboring about six other rescues at the time and I sensed that her husband, John, was pressuring her to get rid of one. Apparently, the beagle (Toby), the newest edition, had disrupted whatever chemistry had existed within the pack.

Marcia lived three miles away in a rustic farmhouse just off the main thoroughfare. When I pulled in, I heard the cacophony of howls, barks, and whimpers as my car rumbled to a stop on the cobblestone driveway.

I walked in with the feeling that I was going to go home with a new beagle. Marcia greeted me, then retreated to a back room where she managed to release just Toby, although all six dogs were desperately trying to nudge their way through the door and into the main room to greet me.

Out he came, his legs spinning along the wooden floor as he desperately tried to secure his footing. The exuberance in seeing a new face only intensified the furor of his advance and he skidded head first into the sofa. Dazed for a moment, and panting furiously, he gathered himself and then sat up on his hind legs and howled at me.

Oh, God. That's what Barney used to do. And he looked exactly like Barney. Well, almost. His coloring was virtually identical, although he lacked a tiny white strip on his forehead. Instead, there was a kind of crevice or dent in his head, a place my son would later say was where they were supposed to put his brains. And he was a big beagle, fifteen inches high, not eleven like many beagles. Just like Barney.

And he had the eyes. He had Barney's eyes. Marcia knew I was hooked. I knew I was hooked. Even the dog knew it.

We struck a deal. I'd take Toby home for the weekend, introduce him to Mary Ellen, Brett, and Benson, and if we could get through Saturday and Sunday without structural damage to the house or major opposition from feline or family, I'd take him.

Toby jumped in the car and we took off for his new home, but before we departed Marcia saddled me with one piece of additional information about the dog. He had been a stray, which I knew, but when Marcia took him to the vet they discovered a microchip in his neck. This is often a good sign of a vigilant, caring owner. Marcia had tried to contact the family, but they had not returned repeated calls.

The last thing I wanted to do was bond with the dog, then have to return him. I had a flashback to the early days of Barney's celebrity when people would come up to me and claim that Barney belonged to them and until they had seen him on TV, they had no idea what had happened to their precious little (fill in any name). Most folks were just pulling one of our six legs, but it did raise a frightening specter of how I would have dealt with a serious challenge to my ownership.

Toby dragged me into the house, a good indication of my challenges ahead. It was about 2 PM, so Brett was still at school; Mary Ellen was at work. Toby sniffed about but was decidedly reserved, a touch skittish in his new surroundings. Suddenly, a cameo appearance by Benson, who simply eyeballed the dog and confirmed it was Barney—suggesting that reports of the beagle's death had been exaggerated. Then as Benson moved on, he got the first delayed whiff of the intruder, just nanoseconds after the initial visual ID. This was enough to dissuade him of his original assessment. His head whipped around to scrutinize Toby. Wait! One more quick look. Hey, that's not Barney. What are they trying to pull over on me? Now we had hair on end, growling, paw swatting. A cat hissy fit.

But don't miss the point here. Benson had done a double take, an honest-to-goodness theatrical, Hollywood double take. Even Barney had never mastered that.

It was a tough weekend. Toby clearly possessed all the attributes that would make him a possible substitute for Barney. This meant that he was also a bit incorrigible. Could I make my family go through this again? Did I have to? Remember that I still had not been instructed by the TV station *not* to get another dog. I knew it in my gut, but no one had the nerve to tell me. Yet.

***

We were at a precarious point. We had all cozied up to Toby over those few days—even Brett, although that zeal would wane eventually. But did we really want another beagle? Well, I did. I was hoping this was not going to a household vote.

Within a week, that decision was made crystal clear to me by my boss. Crystal clear! Did I want the truth? Could I handle the truth? "No more dogs," I was told. "Let's face it," said the news director, "there can never be another Barney." You could read that with any inflection you wanted, but here was the bottom line: no more reporters with canine sidekicks. But what about me? Would I continue in the same gig without a dog?

As Cochrun later explained, he felt my value as a reporter on live shots was a waste of my real talent. He was a fan of my weekly newspaper column and wanted me to devote my time to feature packages, stories that are written and edited. "No more live stuff," he said. I panicked. I was flattered he liked my writing, but five produced stories a week meant twice the work. I didn't have to write or edit the live segments. I just did them. It also meant the end of the spontaneous nature of the show. I told my wife I was going to quit. She wasn't a big fan of that idea, so I agreed to try it.

So there would not be another dog. How did I feel about that? I must admit, I have always thought it was the right decision, but for the wrong reason. The boss was correct. There would never be another Barney. Everything about Barney's stardom, his impact on the community, was pure happenstance. He was a one-in-a-billion beagle, thrown into the ideal situation with this aging reporter who was just perceptive enough to capitalize on the pairing, highlighting the antic-prone tendencies of this special canine.

No, there could never be another Barney. But this decree was not about Barney's irreplaceability, it was about getting a new, more "sophisticated" look for the news. That's why they didn't want my live daily shenanigans anymore. The new emphasis would be on news, weather, and traffic.

The truth is that the package segments were a success. I won awards and over forty of my pieces were nationally syndicated. But even that gig bit the dust, finally. Two years later, I was told that viewers didn't have time to watch a thoughtful two-minute segment in the morning. They needed to get the basics and head out the door. Which is where I thought *I* was headed. The solution from the station: Put Wolfsie on live on the weekends. His shtick will sell there. People have more time to watch.

By the time I had been told that Barney was not going to be replaced, Toby had already become a member of the Wolfsie family. It was too late to turn back. We were stuck with him. Crass, I know, but the family choice of a dog—if we were voting—would not have been for a beagle. Mary Ellen had grown up with a collie. That was supposed to be our next dog.

I did have one call to make. I had to make sure that Toby's previous owners—the ones Marcia had traced through Toby's microchip—weren't still looking for him. I called again and this time, damn it, someone answered. I did not reveal my name, which might have been an invitation to sell the dog, rather than relinquish it.

"I found your dog, Ma'am. A beagle, about three, a tri-color, male."

There was silence for several seconds. I asked again if it was her dog.

"He's a pain in the ass. He's trouble," she finally uttered. Little did she know that this was the kind of dog that had made me famous. But wait. Trouble can mean a lot of things. I pushed for details. "Look, there's a lot of tension in my house," she continued. "My husband and I are getting a divorce. And he keeps running away."

"The dog or your husband?"

Forgive me. A straight line of such immense potential could not be ignored. But it worked. She hung up the phone. Toby was mine. I was thrilled. Or was I?

Those first few weeks were like reliving the nightmare of the previous twelve years. He was as bad as Barney in every way. In one way, he was worse. Barney had been housebroken. How and when he acquired that skill, we never knew. But Toby had a whiz-anywhere attitude.

Halloween night, Brett, Mary Ellen, Toby, and I sat at the front of our driveway passing out candy to skeletons, ballerinas, and devils. Toby sat calmly next to us, wagging his tail at every ghost that floated by. Suddenly, as if he had been frightened, he turned and bolted for the front door.

"What's the matter with Toby?" asked a neighbor who had joined our little group. "Why does he want to go back inside?"

"He probably has to go to the bathroom," said Mary Ellen. It was her funniest line of our marriage.

Could Toby have become another Barney? He certainly had all the required bad habits and mischievous inclinations. But as I tell people almost daily, Barney was not something I had planned. True, once he came into my life, I nurtured and enabled the very behavior that made him a household word. But as Lee Giles put it, "You could never have that kind of magic again," which is another way of saying what the great Greek philosopher Heraclitus declared, "You never step in the same river twice." I suppose this is a bad analogy when you are talking about dogs, but when it came to Barney, I could only step in it once.

End of the Tail

Beginning in 2006, I was back on live TV doing remotes on Saturday and Sunday mornings as I had for twelve years with Barney on weekdays. It was still a hoot, but the howl was missing and I still sometimes got the eerie feeling Barney was looking over me, just making sure I was doing something silly.

Every day, viewers came up to me to tell me how much they missed the two of us on the morning news. They still do. And when people saw me with Toby in public they assumed he was a star-in-training, a dog who would jump-start their weekend mornings. "No, he's just my dog. He's not a TV dog," I explained. Most folks just nodded their heads. "You're right, you could never replace Barney." But the notion of having a partner again was hard to let go of. Should there have been a new Barney? Could Toby have filled that role? Would the management at the station have considered a dog on the weekend segments if I had pushed it? What a guy like me doesn't need is something like this to obsess about.

Instead, I found something new to obsess about. I felt the need to capture all my memories of Barney while they were still fresh. But how? Should I write a book? I had already put together a paperback scrapbook that included many of the weekly humor columns I had written about him over the years. But an entire book? Like in some kind of order, with chapters and a theme? This is not what people with ADD do in their spare time.

I wrestled with this dilemma for weeks, while a patient publisher waited for my decision. My good friend and college buddy Mark Olshaker, a writer himself, pushed me to do this. He said my hesitation was just fear of success. My wife said I was afraid of failure. Then my agent called and said he was afraid the deadline for my decision was the next morning at 9.

That afternoon, I picked up *USA Today* and there it was on the front page: Uno, an adorable little beagle, had just won the Westminster Dog Show, the Academy Awards for canines. The accompanying article praised the little pooch, making it clear that a beagle had never won this coveted honor.

I watched Uno on TV all day, interacting with his fans— so full of personality, so full of life. So what was I waiting for? This was a sign, pure and simple. I decided to write this book.

I continued to follow Uno's coronation the next week, watching the coverage over and over again as he captured everyone's heart, just like Barney. Yes, he was best in show, but he also could have won noisiest in show (not to mention nosiest) and the hungriest. No beagle had been in contention before, although back in 2003, there had been a rumor that one was being considered but the owner let him outside for a minute to exercise and he didn't come back for three months.

One of Uno's biggest rivals was a poodle named Vicki, who apparently had her own video on YouTube. I wish that such Internet opportunities had been available when I had Barney. I would have started a Web site called MyMess.com, a place where beagle owners could post photos of the destruction their hounds wreaked that day, as well as where they were last seen before wandering off.

From the TV exposure he received after the victory, we learned a great deal about Uno. He loved having his picture taken, for example. "He just eats that up," said his owner. Barney felt the same way about publicity. But he devoured the pictures. And two lens caps and a leather carrying case.

Prior to this event, Uno had already won several ribbons, all of which I am sure he buried in the backyard. Beagles really aren't impressed with awards. In 2002, the winning dog was a German shorthair pointer. I could imagine her spending all day indicating to people with her paw that her ribbon was above the mantel.

At the announcement that Uno had won, poodles stuck up their noses, Shar-Peis rolled their eyes (we assume), and Afghans, who were already suffering from some bad international press, were unimpressed. Beagles, you see, are kind of a lunch-bucket dog. When they came to America, they came to work, not to sit on someone's lap or lounge on a Persian rug. I'm more liberal on immigration than most politicians but seeing some of these exotic dogs at Westminster made me think maybe we should have a fence around the U.S. border. Not that this would stop a beagle, but it might deter Irish setters, who would simply crash head-first into the barrier.

Uno made me realize there was more to tell about Barney and I was sure that after his victory, a whole new decade of beagles would be around every corner and in every garbage can. Uno's demeanor on TV in the following days was a giant billboard for hounds looking for homes. Just like *1001 Dalmatians* catapulted that breed to new popularity, beagle adoptions rose in 2007–08. For those of you who went out and got a beagle after Uno won, this book is a confirmation of the love and loyalty you have no doubt enjoyed. And some of the hassles you have endured.

If you are still deciding what kind of dog you want, let this be a loving word of warning.

A Final Word

In August 1991, I was outside the recently closed state mental hospital just west of downtown Indy, waiting to do an interview with the state health commissioner. Barney was on a long leash attached to the telephone pole when a Volkswagen bus rounded the corner. Barney darted into the street in pursuit of a squirrel. Marcus Collins, the first photographer assigned to Barney and me, yanked on his leash, pulling the beagle back from the intersection. The VW whizzed by, missing the beagle by a hair.

No yank in history (other than Mickey Mantle) would so affect my life. I just didn't realize it then. It was too early in the career of this rising canine star.

Barney and I would spend the next twelve years together. The number may not sound that impressive but consider this: During a similar length of time I somehow skated past junior high, wisecracked my way through high school, and negotiated four years of college. Let's throw in two years of grad school. At the time of Barney's death, he had been with me half the length of my twenty-four-year marriage and most of my son's life.

It was twelve years filled with ups and downs: in relationships with family, friends and coworkers, as well as in the stock market. My son went from toddler to teenager.

And there was 9/11.

Wall-to-wall media coverage followed that horrific event and thus a moratorium was imposed by management on my daily segment with Barney. In light of the tragedy, airing our antics might have struck viewers as frivolous and inappropriate. We both sat it out. The two weeks following the attack were the longest time that Barney and I did not do our thing on TV. Both of us sat on the bench.

In a way, people needed the diversion we provided, maybe more than ever. But all of us in the media had a hard time deciding what was a respectful way to grieve, relieve the stress, and cover the news. There was no recent precedent in any newsroom.

The first day back on the air, I explained our absence. Then, somehow, it was business as usual for the next two years, up until Barney's death. I really believe that the beagle helped all of us in some small way handle the difficult months that followed the tragedy.

Barney was always my rock. While his behavior was unpredictable, his role in my life and others' lives never varied. He woke up next to me every morning, then he trotted off to work with me. His role was simple: Be himself. Ignore the rules. Have fun. See you again tomorrow.

At the beginning of this man-and-his-dog story, I sometimes I wondered if I really wanted to be identified, not as talk-show host, or a reporter, or a writer, but instead, as Barney's dad. That insecurity evaporated quickly as I saw the impact Barney made on the community. I will never know if a different dog could have gotten the job down. Maybe

Barney wondered if he had picked a different TV personality if things would have worked out quite so well.

I will be linked forever with Barney. When people bring up Barney's antics, I take pride in what we did together. My license plate for the last seventeen years, BARNEY 8, is in more ways than one moving proof of that. I am now less recognizable without the dog. There was a time it bothered me a little if people remembered Barney's name and not mine.

No longer . . .

"Hey, weren't you the guy with Barney on TV?"

"Yes, I was. Thanks for watching."

Here's the bottom line: Without Barney, I would have still gotten plenty of laughs, acquired a few loyal fans, and maybe even racked up a few awards. But I wouldn't have captured a single heart.

There's a little beagle in all of us—yearning to try something new, searching for an adventure with hope that along the way we can touch a few lives.

Thanks, Barney, thanks from all of us.

Acknowledgments

This book was written entirely from my head . . . and heart. I never had to go to the library, never surfed the Internet or Googled anything. So unlike some authors who wax on about their research assistants and experts who collaborated on their manuscript, I don't have to.

My good friend and fellow writer Mark Olshaker encouraged me, actually coerced me, into writing this book, and provided his professional guidance every step along the way. Mark had more confidence in my ability than I did. That's the best kind of friend to have.

Then there is my wife, Mary Ellen, who said that if I didn't write the book, I'd probably end up hating myself. She was right. That's also what she said about my first ten books. Heidi Newman, my personal editor, never caved until I rewrote every sentence she hated. There were lots of them.

Thanks to Shawn Coyne, my agent, for recognizing a good story and believing in it. My gratitude goes to Ann Treistman, my editor at Skyhorse publishing, for her insightful suggestions and patience in helping to make this book a reality.

And, of course, I extend my most profound appreciation to the tens of thousands of Barney fans who still tell me how much they miss him. They are not only the reason I wrote the book, but they are the reason there was a story to share in the first place.